# An English Amateur
# in Antarctica

# An English Amateur in Antarctica

---

MARTIN BURTON

NEW EUROPEAN PUBLICATIONS  LONDON

Published in the United Kingdom in 2004 by
**New European Publications Limited**
14-16 Carroun Road
London SW8 1JT, England

British Library Cataloguing in Publication Data

ISBN  1-872410-43-X

Designed & typeset by studio@orbitgraphic.co.uk
Set in Monotype Dante

Printed and bound in Great Britain by Antony Rowe, Chippenham, Wiltshire.

To my parents
who gave me freedom as a child,
and
Christina, Isabel and Marina
who have supported all my travels

I would like to thank Ronny Finsaas and
Geoff Somers for their photographs

 # St Thomas ' Lupus Trust

There can be few diseases that strike more fear in the hearts of patients and doctors alike. Lupus – an "unknown" disease and a "small print" disease – often strikes at young people in the prime of life. The older textbooks painted a picture of doom and gloom – "untreatable", "fatal" – a great "mimic", going undiagnosed or wrongly diagnosed for months or even years.

Mercifully, in the past 30 years things have dramatically changed for the better. Lupus is now recognised as being common – up to one in 800 females in some studies – more common, for example, than multiple sclerosis or leukaemia. Fortunately, research into the causes and treatment of lupus is bringing rewards as it becomes far more effective.

Finding the money to fund research is never easy. Some ten years ago we decided to set up our own charity, the St Thomas' Lupus Trust. This charity, for which we all work, now supports the clinical and laboratory work of our unit, and has proved "life-saving" to our research effort.

It was through our first fundraiser, Barbara Osborn, severely affected with a form of lupus, that Martin Burton became involved, first as a supporter and then as a Trustee.

Martin has galvanised our Trust. His energy in helping to raise money for the St Thomas' Lupus Trust is prodigious. That he should have succeeded in his "mid-life" trek from the South Pole came as no surprise to all of us working in the lupus unit.

Thank you Martin for channelling your fantastic energy and drive into helping patients with lupus.

**Graham Hughes**
*Head*, Lupus Unit
St Thomas' Hospital

*All revenues from this book to go to St Thomas' Lupus Trust.*

# Contents

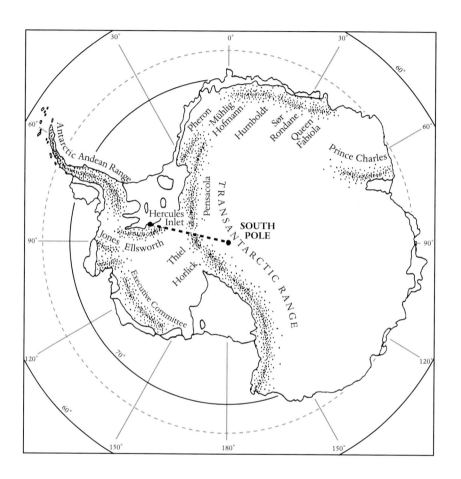

# Preface

The title *An English Amateur in Antarctica* conjures up the image of an ordinary person doing an rather extraordinary thing. This book is the story of an extraordinary person doing a very extraordinary thing in a totally extraordinary place.

In my business of raising money for expeditions one often has to go the extra step.

I first met Martin Burton when I was about to embark on a *Wadwalk* across the sea in Holland.

This entails walking, often chest high in saltwater, for 10 miles through clinging mud up to the knees, such fun. The purpose was to give some City of London types an experience, and in return for the experience they were expected to give my Mission Antarctica Foundation a healthy donation.

I saw Martin at the start, and to be honest thought that with his rather robust frame, at the time, he would not make it a mile, never mind ten miles. There was, however, a gleam in his eye which I put down to fear, not determination.

As I was staggering along at the back, I never saw Martin for the entire walk . At the end I came across him and was informed that he had been leading for most of the way. Trust me, that was very hard work indeed.

I learnt a lesson about Martin that day; never underestimate the man.

Reading these pages you feel Martin's determination and humility.

You will read how I and others in the Polar world let him down with empty gestures and promises, but this did not deter him and he continued on with his plan.

You will discover how he kept his focus and did what he said he was going to do.

Today it is possible to fly near to the South Pole and make a short journey of perhaps sixty miles to *experience* that marvellous place.

Martin, with two team members, chose to make the full journey of nearly seven hundred statute miles from the Pole to the first sea ice. This is a special achievement, and ranks him, for what it is worth, with a very select few.

*If you can do, or dream you can,*
*begin it now for boldness has genius,*
*power and magic in it*

**FAUST, *Johann Wolfgang von Goethe***

*John Anster in his 1835 translation of Faust*

That is the story.
With all respect to Martin
Truly

**Robert Swan  OBE**

# 1

## Friday, December 5, 2003

The temperature was thirty below zero, visibility was poor, and I kept falling over. I had been a skier for twenty-eight years and had never fallen over as many times as I was doing today. I had been on the trail since 6.45 the previous evening and it was some hours after midnight. We had chosen to ski sail through the night, so we always had the sun behind us and not in our eyes. It was a tough day, with little wind, and I was reduced to virtually man-hauling my sledge.

I could see my two companions a long way ahead of me, waiting patiently as I fell over again, this time in a bundle which left me half-trapped between the sledge I was towing and the 50 metre lines of the kite I was using to find some force in the light wind to increase my speed. I was constantly fearful of being injured in one of the falls, because the ice-surface, the *sastrugi*, was hard, with peaks and troughs of between one and three feet. If I did require a rescue, it was not a surface that an aircraft could land on.

In the past two hours I had covered just over half a nautical mile. In the next half-hour I travelled a hundred yards. All distances were measured in nautical miles, 6,000 feet; 60 nautical miles is equal to one degree of latitude that close to the South Pole, 22 miles south of us. We dreamed of doing a "One-Degree Day", 60 miles in the 10 hours between 7 o'clock in the evening when we started ski sailing, and our stop time, 5 o'clock in the morning. We were 9,500 feet up on the Antarctic plateau, heading north. All directions were north from the South Pole, but we were trying to follow the line of longitude 86 degrees west. The way the wind blew, along with my inexperience of kiting with skis, meant we were drifting further west, as far out as 92 degrees west.

I pulled myself back on to my feet, and sorted out the two stiff poles – called Pulk arms – attached from my waist to the sledge. The way I had fallen this time, my skis were trapped and the sledge fell on top of me. Both the Pulk arms were digging into my suspect back. Every time I fell over I knew that I was risking an injury. Normally I tried not to think about this. Out of earshot of my companions, there was no incentive to sound cool or keep a poker face, and I vented my feelings by swearing.

Earlier that morning, using a sail instead of a kite, we had covered four miles in two hours. This was not a huge distance, but it was a great deal better than kiting half a mile in two hours. To get from the South Pole to Hercules Inlet, a distance of 607 miles (698 statute miles), we had allocated ourselves thirty food days. Hercules Inlet was the nearest sea ice to the South Pole, and the three of us were ski sailing or ski kiting our way there; we needed to cover an average of 20 miles a day. This was day two, and on day one in a first leg we all agreed was opportunist, catching a real wind at the Pole itself, we had covered 16.2 miles. It was an absolute certainty that today was going to put us even more behind the average.

Aside from the light winds, I was the main reason for the delay. It was my first full day ever of using a kite to travel on skis, and I was having difficulty travelling at more than 250 yards in an hour.

Learning to kite was hard work if I was not doing it properly. It was harder work, I discovered, doing it badly than it was when I was doing it properly, if I could ever reach that happy state. I was always on catch-up.

Had this been a training session, the sort of sessions I had gone through learning how to ski with sails, there would have been a hotel nearby. I knew if that was the case I would opt not to kite any more and retire to the bar and a good dinner, and perhaps return the following day. But I did not have that option. I just had to keep getting up and being pulled down again, and getting up and being pulled down again.

Four hundred yards ahead of me, nearly ninety minutes away at the speed I was moving over the *sastrugi*, Geoff Somers and Ronny Finsaas watched me. I could not see the horizon, but I could see them. It spurred me on, still swearing, to get my kite in the air and start travelling once more.

I covered a few yards and then fell over again.

Geoff, 52, an Englishman from Keswick in Cumbria, had radioed Patriot Hills that morning, saying he had never seen the *sastrugi* so bad so close to the Pole. He told me he had loosened his ski bindings to a minimum, because he feared a fall would break a leg where no aerial rescue was possible. I had felt that a ski coming off at speed was the more likely cause of an accident, and kept my bindings tight. I had little experience of travelling in Polar regions, nothing compared to Geoff, one of the world's best Polar travellers. He had six times led groups to the North Pole, and was a veteran of the first and only traverse of the Antarctic Continent by its greatest axis, a seven-month journey of nearly 4,000 miles. Geoff was my guide and Polar navigator. He never showed any sympathy, then or later, about the plight I was in. I was not certain I ever knew what he was really thinking.

Ronny Finsaas, a 30-year-old Norwegian, was my guest on the journey. He had years of experience at ski sailing and kiting, and had chosen to live in a tiny village called Finse next to the Hardangervissa, probably the best ski sailing area in Norway, purely so he could spend most of his life ski sailing and watching wildlife. This was his first trip out of Norway. He was a chef by profession – though we had no experience yet of his skills with the boil-in-a-bag meals we were eating every evening – and had spent the last six years pushing the limits of ski sailing. Ronny had once travelled at 50 mph pulling a sledge, and sailed 30 miles in the dark in two hours, using a headlamp and a GPS, the global positioning system instrument that has revolutionised Polar navigation.

Geoff and Ronny had told me in one of the infrequent times I caught up with them that I would get the hang of kiting. I dearly hoped so.

My body was holding up quite well, but there were already signs of deterioration. My fingers were cracked around the nails, even though I had an option of four separate pairs of gloves, one fitting on top of another. The best hand protection were mitts made of down, and I raided my sledge when my hands became too cold to slip them into the mitts and get feeling back. But I could not kite with the mitts, and the kite was the only way, with the winds so light, to get any help propelling my laden sledge over the rough surface.

My left foot was slightly swollen, and I was treating it with anti-inflammatory cream and favouring it slightly. The constant battering of the *sastrugi*, and being caught between the force of the kite pulling me forwards and the surface constantly holding me back, meant my knees felt like they had been pushing at a piston engine for two days. I faced the prospect of up to 28 days of similar effort ahead of me. Fortunately, my back was holding up, despite months of pain caused by over-training This was thanks to an hour's work a few days earlier by a blind Chilean masseur I had found at the back of a hairdresser's shop in Punta Arenas. Two of my teeth, both implants, had fallen out on the flight down from London, and I had had them glued back in again in Santiago. Now we were actually on the ice in freezing temperatures, which rendered the chocolate I ate daily almost as hard as rock, all my teeth stayed in my mouth. I was grateful for small mercies.

I got to my feet again, more swearing, more sorting out the harness to pull the sledge, more getting the kite in the air, a few more yards covered and I fell over again.

My companions were getting cold waiting, but at no time that day did they complain. They remained watching, Ronny eating nuts and chocolate, Geoff eating nothing; he never ate during the day.

I struggled up again, longing to find within me the skills I felt I had using sails for propulsion, with lines just 20 feet long and utilising surface winds, compared with the 150 foot lines of a kite, designed to find lift and power a hundred feet above the ice surface. Ronny, the kiting expert, had said that when I learned how to use a kite I would do it by feel. But while learning, I had to look up all the time to see what the kite was doing, and I could not at the same time look down and make judgements about the best surface of the *sastrugi* to ski over.

In kiting, control of the lines was by flexible handles. The handles changed the aspect ratio of the kite to the wind, effectively opening and closing its face. My attachment to the kite included a loop that came through a pulley, all part of keeping control, but it left me entirely at the mercy of the wind. Even when the wind was light it required strength to pull the handles, tracing figures of eight to pull the wind into the kite and move forward. With its long lines a kite was more dangerous than a sail, and there was less control if a gust of wind blew up, a common event in the Antarctic. I was attached to the kite by a harness around my stomach, and to avoid being tossed like a rag doll between the forces of kite and sledge, I would have to unhook myself and let it go. Sooner or later the kite snagged on the *sastrugi*, forcing me to untangle all its long lines. The longer the lines, the more time it took to sort out.

It was not just the falling over. Another problem was making progress and then finding strong resistance from the sledge. When I looked back it had rolled over, no longer on runners, and the drag greatly increased. That meant bringing the kite down without snagging, unclipping the Pulk arms, righting the sledge again, and getting back into harness.

The sledges of Ronny and Geoff did not turn over as regularly as mine, and I had tried skiing in their tracks to get the same "luck" as they had. I kept asking myself, what was wrong with my technique? If I followed in their tracks and theirs did not turn over, surely mine would not turn over either? I soon came to the conclusion that this was cheating, and offended a puritanical ethic I had not realised, in this instance, that I had. With all the surface of Antarctica to ski over, why should I have to pick on the tracks made in virgin snow by my companions? It was not enough to answer: "So I don't fall over". I wanted to kite without falling over, and I dearly wished not to be the weakest member of the three, even though I was the only amateur between two professionals.

I had not wanted to show any weakness when we were resting, and I was still burning with the thought of Geoff's reaction the previous evening when I had asked for three extra inches in the tent so I could put my coffee cup down. I had had those three inches the first night we shared the tent at the South Pole, and when I did not get that space, the only place to put my drink, the following evening, I asked for it again. Ronny, in the middle position, said nothing, but at

5

the far end of the tent where Geoff did the cooking, my demand had been met with derision. Geoff had to find room where he was cooking for all three of us, and he risked burning his bedding if the safety shield on the spirit cooker failed. He did not take kindly to my demand for the extra three inches. I had privately resolved never again to ask for extra space within the tent, and to take what I was given.

I had also resolved not to be weak when we were moving, however slowly. I had paid the expenses of all three of us on the journey, more than two hundred thousand dollars worth, without any help from the usual sponsors who back Polar trips. This did not mean I wanted to be pampered. I saw myself, and I hoped my companions felt the same way, as an equal member of the team, and not someone who was the guv'nor, who needed extra support.

I felt this way despite Ronny suggesting an hour earlier that I should reduce the weight of my sledge, on a rare time when I caught up with the other two and before they turned and raced ahead of me. It was obvious that my poor kiting technique was slowing us up, and Ronny felt he could pull more, and give me a lighter load. I passed over one of my holdalls, and felt no dishonour doing this, despite my acute sense of what was and what was not dishonour. After all, I carried as a visible proof of my sense of honour a coat of arms on the back of my sledge, which I resolutely wished to stay with me through the journey. We had agreed that as a team we would make faster progress if I had less resistance in my sledge. But Ronny struggled with the extra load in the light wind, progress did not improve and so I took my holdall back.

I had expected to use sails with my skis on this journey, but not kites. It was Ronny who decided we each needed a kite as well, especially to get away from the South Pole on the high plateau of ice where the winds were often light or calm. Two years earlier, there had been an expensive failure when two travellers had set off with the same goal as us. Because they did not have kites and the winds were light, they did not get away from the Pole, and had to be rescued. All our insurance premiums had gone up steeply as a result of this incident. It was only actually being there and seeing the conditions one-to-one, travelling within those conditions, that the necessity for kiting skills was brought home to me.

*Leaving the Pole, sastrugi immediately creates problems for sledges.* © *Ronny Finsaas*

*Geoff in front avoiding some larger sastrugi.*

*Conditions deteriorating. Ronny releases his sledge to return to Geoff.*

*Long kite lines with 30 metres and 20 metres joined for very light winds.*
©Ronny Finsaas

*Ronny using his 10 sqm sail.*

*Some occasional soft snow on the plateau.*

*Another sledge roll.* © *Ronny Finsaas*

*Gusting winds take Martin Burton's skis off the ice.* © *Ronny Finsaas*

We each had three sails, the biggest, 14 SqM – square metres – for the lightest winds, through a 10 SqM sail to the smallest, 5 SqM when there was a good wind blowing. If it was calm we could not move at all. For winds between calm and 5/6 mph, a kite was necessary. This was the first day I had seriously used one. I did not count the two hours at my home in Surrey that autumn when I played with a sample kite before it ended up in a tree and I sent the remains back to Ronny in Norway, the sail intact, the lines still decorating the branches. When I thought about using a kite I had just hoped it would not become necessary, and if it did, I would learn. Geoff had said there would be the opportunity to learn to kite on the plateau because the ground would be flat, ideal circumstances to learn how to ski kite. That is what I was doing, learning, and the process was both painful and humiliating. I hated holding up Geoff and Ronny. They may have said nothing critical to me, but I was saying a great deal critically to myself.

It never crossed my mind to stop and abandon the journey. Good things happen and bad things happen, but if I kept going, good things would start to happen. It was like spinning a coin. The odds were the same the following day. Just because it was bad today did not mean it would be good tomorrow. We could be many weeks on the ice, and we did not know what was going to happen. I knew it was a mental game as well as a physical game. I just had to keep going.

I was mentally prepared for not wanting to like where I was. Indeed, that was almost mandatory. I knew I could not complete this journey without pain. The question was, how much pain? Whatever it was, I was going to put up with it. What was the whole journey worth if it was not a struggle? I cannot say I enjoyed the struggle, especially while it was going on, but there was no question of despair.

It was only a question of getting through.

We had factored in the light winds and knew we would not be travelling fast on the plateau, but personally I had not anticipated that we would travel slowly because of poor snow conditions. Later, when we dropped down thousands of feet, we hoped for the wind to return and the ice surface to improve, and thought we could make much bigger daily distances than 20 miles.

But the Antarctic was not our servant, and would do to us whatever transpired. We were committed to living with that and surviving and if possible winning through.

Despite yet another fall I nursed the opinion of my companions to my chest that I would eventually pick up kiting techniques. I felt sure I would, although it did not feel like it on the day. The fact that they were so far ahead of me physically created its own pressure and emphasised my status as the weakest member of the team. Each time I caught up with them, they had already rested and turned and headed north. I never got a rest. I had to just keep going. It seemed like forever.

We did not do ten hours travelling that day. Instead of going through until 5 o'clock in the morning, we packed up early, at 2 o'clock. That was 7 ¼ hours altogether, of which 2 ¾ hours were with a kite.

I was personally more exhausted than the others.

Setting up camp, we fell into a routine of doing certain jobs. All three of us worked at setting up the tent, which took about ten minutes. Geoff went inside and arranged our mats and sleeping bags, setting them out in our designated places, and got the stove going for hot water. Ronnie and I protected the tent by digging a snow wall around it, using shovels. Ronnie always got the ice for the water. He had a saw, and cut off some *sastrugi*, pure wonderful clean water. Ronnie would give it to Geoff to melt. Typically, I would do the majority of digging the snow. I took it that if there was technique required, Geoff did it. If it was manual, it was my job.

I deliberately took my time to prepare my own sledge. I did not want to get into the tent too early. I wanted to leave Geoff room to move around there and establish himself. There was no hurry for me. By the time I crawled into the tent, I was always the last one in.

I had a satellite phone with me and phoned my wife Christina to tell her about our progress. Her cousin Jan answered the phone and told me Christina was out shopping. I had tried phoning my wife the previous day, and my 14-year old daughter Marina had answered, also saying her mum was out. It was only much later I discovered that Christina was in hospital, but did not want the news to get through to me in case it caused me to abandon the journey.

We had travelled 8.6miles that day, a total of 8 miles in 5 hours under sail, and 0.6 miles in 2 ¾ hours with a kite. Our cumulative distance from the Pole was 24.6 miles.

We would eat salami waiting for our dinner, but I did not bother doing that. I got into my sleeping bag, intending to wake up when the boil-in-a-bag food was ready. I thought I would doze off and awake for dinner.

Instead I collapsed and went to sleep, and slept all night.

In all my utter exhaustion, cold hands and feet, anger and frustration at not being able to use a kite properly, I was still where I wanted to be.

The worse things were, physically, the more I held to that belief.

# 2

# The Smell of Money

My family was no different than any other close working class family. I was a
Boxing Day baby, born in 1953. My father, one of three children, was a postman,
and we lived in South London. I was the elder of two: I have a much younger
sister, Jayne.

I was brought up in a house in a *cul-de-sac* with my grandparents as well
as my parents, and two aunts lived in the same road. My dad brought home his
wages every week to hand to my mother, and she gave him whatever pocket
money was available. This was in sharp contrast to many working class families
where wives did not always know what their husbands earned. My dad played a
straight bat, and did not go out gambling or spending the money before he gave
over his pay packet. Because funds were limited, it came down to the family first
and he took out of it whatever was left for him to have. As such, he was not able
to take risks in his life. He put everything into the family.

I grew up questioning why he never took any risks. But I also appreciated
that the great advantage about my parents playing a low-risk game in providing

a happy family base, that it enabled me to take risks. I have taken risks in both my business and my personal life, always knowing that even if there was nothing else out there, there was still the safe environment of my parents. That was a strong influence on me, and it still is.

I went through my first seventeen years without the smell of money. It is not possible to describe to those who have never smelled money just what that smell is, but when I first came across it I knew immediately what it was.

In those days about six children in a hundred in England went to university; now it is thirty per cent, including my two daughters. I was not one of the six percent, though I was a keen sportsman at school. One of my sports was lacrosse, in which I played for the south of England; as not many people play lacrosse, it is probably not a great feat. I did some running, and played cricket for Surrey Colts, and football for the South London Boys.

I left school at sixteen. My first job was as a hod carrier on a building site. Then, to better myself – it would have been said then – I started work in a surveyor's office, aiming to become a chartered surveyor. I hated it. It was not just the job that was boring, all the people doing it were boring. They were not doing a job that any of them appeared to like.

At seventeen I had long hair and a motorbike, and I had come to a decision to save as much money as I could and travel the world. I liked looking at atlases, especially the pink bits all over the world that had once been ours. I felt proud of the British Empire. But the parts that were especially interesting, such as Antarctica and the other ice cap around the Arctic and Greenland, often fell off the globe.

I knew there were not many people there, which was also attractive.

To make extra money I was serving at a petrol station. It was not self-service then and I was expected to talk to customers, always looking for ways to sell them oil. One day a customer asked me what the price of his petrol would be. Like many drivers, he did not know what he was going to pay until the sums had been put into the till. But when I knew how much petrol he wanted, and told him immediately what he had to pay, he was impressed.

"You should be working in the City," he said.

Arithmetic was second nature to me. The customer said he was a partner at a firm of jobbers called Bisgood Bishop, and he gave me his phone number and said to contact him. At that time I did not know what a jobber was. However impressed I may have been with his offer, I was still seventeen years of age, and I did not take kindly to his parting remark.

"Obviously, you'll have to have a haircut," he said.

As a result, I did not call him.

He came back a month later, and said, "You haven't rung me. How dare you!"

"No, you're right," I said, realising the opportunity, "I will call you".

I had two haircuts, because I could not bring myself to do it all in one go to look respectable. Then I took the money I had saved to go around the world and bought a suit. It was my first suit, and I knew I needed one for the interview. I reasoned at the time that there were two ways to go around the world. The first way was to do it as a very young man with little money and living out of a rucksack. The second way was to make a lot of money and pay to travel. It was with this thought in mind that I set off to see the office manager at Bisgood Bishop.

When I walked through the doors of Bisgood Bishop, I smelled money. Having been brought up fairly poor, it was something special to smell. I had never smelled money before. I was committed.

I decided immediately that I wanted to keep smelling it.

I started at Bisgood Bishop on October 4, 1971. My position as a jobber's clerk was right at the bottom of the pecking order. I was expected to pick up things, to learn by watching, to be sharp and avoid a bollocking. There were no formal courses and certificates. I either won through to the next highest job – a red button checking the paperwork of the jobbers making deals – or I got the push. The next rank above a red button was a blue button, a boy's job – girls were not allowed to do it until much later in the 1970s, they were all boys' jobs – physically linking the brokers who asked for the price of deals, and the jobbers who actually quoted prices. That meant walking the floor of the Stock Exchange, looking for the best deal.

I was not a very good jobber's clerk, and also not particularly good at being a red button, a checking clerk, but the company stuck with me. It was fifteen months before I got the opportunity to be a blue button, and I just took to it. Trading was where I found my vocation, closer to the actual smell of money than checking deals, one step away from the deals themselves.

Being aware was everything. I was expected to listen to all the deals going on, and be conscious before anyone else of the way markets were moving. Moods could change quickly between buying and selling. Getting to read the trends correctly could lead me on to where – I now knew – I wanted to be, doing the deals myself. I was successful at that.

In those days, the youngest one could be a dealer was 20, and on my 20th birthday I became a dealer. The youngest one could become a member of the London Stock Exchange was 21, and I was a member of the LSE at 21. I became a partner at Bisgood Bishop at the age of 22, within 4 ½ years of joining.

I had a rapid rise because I put a lot of effort into the job. I did not take holidays, and gave up sports, including lacrosse. The only sporting activity I kept was skiing. Of the partners I joined, most of the new ones were in their mid-30s, and there were senior partners of retirement age, in their late 50s and 60s.

I started my dealing career in the thick of the great Bear period in the London market in 1974, when the FT 30 Index, the precursor to the FTSE 100 Index, dropped to 146. As a young man, obviously with no experience, I thought this was a normal trading market, in which the object remained to make more money than the next man. There may not have been a lot of money around, but to me, even though everything was falling in value, the smell of money remained.

As a new dealer, I made money in the bear market, which made a lasting impression. Most markets are bull markets, where prices go up first, and then maybe later go down. I have always been more comfortable selling shares first before buying them. It is a distinct attitude of mind.

I became interested in options and derivatives, trading the right to buy or sell equities and bonds. I was always interested in new ideas, and I felt that options would be the coming fashion, but there was not much derivatives trading in London at that time. When the CBOE – Chicago Board of Options Exchange – opened, I went over to Chicago in 1975 to see how it worked. In 1978, an options exchange was set up in London, and I wanted to trade on

Bisgood's behalf. Sadly, it was a modest introduction to the market and we could not generate enough income from the business. After nine months I went back to being a jobber, back to the position I used to hold. Bisgood closed down the derivatives business in 1982, a couple of years after I left it. When we sold the whole business to NatWest, they wanted to have a derivatives function, so I offered to re-start it for them. I set up their derivatives operation in 1985, and left fifteen months later.

I had stayed with Bisgood Bishop for fifteen years, not a long time in one company in the City in those days. I was a director of the company when we sold the whole Bisgood business to County Bank, part of the NatWest Group, but left them in May 1986. Two colleagues came with me; we were headhunted as a team. Between us we went to run trading operations for Citicorp on the equity side of the business in London. I ran the derivatives end.

Derivatives sound risky, but the business we were doing was the reverse of risk. We could actually control our positions far better than by not using derivatives.

By now the City had become a key part of my life. I met Christina, my wife, who worked in the City as a stockbroker's clerk, and married her in 1981. We have two daughters, Isabel in December, 1984 and Marina in January, 1989, and I was able to provide a comfortable life for them.

In the late 1980s, working in a senior position for one of the biggest financial institutions in the world was exciting, and I learnt a lot. That was good, but Citicorp itself had problems. The company had to downsize its balance sheet, jargon for making cutbacks, cutting a staff of ten thousand people in Europe back to three thousand. I had become the Managing Director of UK and European Trading for Equities and Derivatives by then, and while I stayed with them I had to make many of the decisions about who stayed and who went.

The downsizing coincided with another momentous time in stockmarket history, the Great Crash in October 1987. Because I had started by trading in 1974 as a Bear, we were always a Bear, and while millions of people were losing shedloads of money when stock prices fell, we made money. For us it was a good period, but it was not enough for us to survive.

I have learned over the years that banks, *especially* banks, always compare themselves with their national competitors when making a judgement. NatWest cared about what Barclays did, Citicorp cared what Chase did and maybe what some of the investment banks like Salomon's were doing. Salomon's did not have a good time over that period, and made a lot of people redundant in December 1987. In Citicorp, as a result, the London office got a directive from New York, where the view was that the climate would deteriorate. New York told us to "reduce our headcount", more jargon for sacking people. It was the beginning of a demoralising period. For a lot of people in Citicorp's London office, the reward for making money was redundancy.

By January 1990, still wearing the Citicorp shirt wholeheartedly, I had put in a lot of effort into making them money. They paid me well, and I performed well. But there were decisions taken in New York that I did not agree with. I felt unable to work for another bank, because I could see that I might possibly be in a similar position again.

I did not normally allow people to screw me more than once.

I started to look for the opportunity to get out.

The screwing was mental. While I was well-rewarded financially, mentally I disliked not being able to control my own destiny. Even though we were a leading London house at the time, we were unable to control our own future. I did not ever want to be in that position again.

The only way to avoid that happening was to start my own business.

I remained on good terms with Citicorp, and set up on my own by buying a small business from them as the platform for my own present company, Monument Securities. The original business employed eight or nine people, which is the number I started with. Obviously I would not have taken this step if there had not been support from clients I had worked with over the years, who were still prepared to trade with me.

By 1993, at the age of 40, I was conscious that I had put all the energies of my life into work. Being independent meant I was my own master. I came to believe that to have freedom, the prerequisite was money, and retaining that freedom meant gathering a certain amount of wealth. Twenty-three years after that Bisgood Bishop jobber drove into the garage where I was working, I started to dream again, as I had dreamed when I was seventeen years old. The dream of travelling the world on my own terms came back to me.

The one sporting activity I had kept up through those working years was skiing. From the age of 22 onwards I went skiing several times a year, nearly always in Europe. If I travelled anywhere, I wanted to use my skis. But wherever I went until 1993, all the journeys had been a compromise between going on my own, or where my family, my wife and daughters, wanted to go. Because of the way I now lived, that restricted the travelling I wanted to do, though I did find some time to be able to travel and ski, broadly in the way that I wanted to. All my activities were driven by the fact that I had a family, a business to run and only a certain amount of time that I could take off.

A lot of effort goes into marriages. I am still married after 23 years of risk-taking, both in business and life, and this is important to me. In the same way as it is probably harder now to play centre-forward for Arsenal than it was 30 or 40 years ago, it is harder to keep a marriage together than it used to be. Life has become more professional. To succeed is more difficult than it used to be, and the whole environment we are in puts more pressure on us than it used to. We do not, for example, now live in a road where there are aunts and uncles.

All events have a trigger point.

For the Antarctic and me, it was supplied in early 1994, by an opinionated Australian.

I had been skiing in Chamonix, in France, and had had a particularly good weekend. This is one of the best European resorts with good backcountry skiing, but the snow and weather had also been perfect, and I had said so at my local pub in the village. This cut little ice with the Australian I was talking to, an airline pilot who also lived in my village. Like many Australians he was opinion-ated about rugby and cricket, and we were accustomed to hearing his views whether we wanted to or not. He had a habit of crowing over Australian victories, especially over the English, but I had not heard his views on skiing before.

He suggested that he did not think much of my views on Chamonix, that by inference he knew more about skiing than I did, and that Chamonix was shit compared to the Lebanon.

I did not even question whether he did know more or not. I just determined to find out first-hand if he was right by going to the Lebanon, so I could actually come to my own opinion. Within ten days I had obtained a visa and set off for Beirut. This was in February 1994, and hostages like Terry Waite and John McCarthy had been released years earlier, but the local Lebanese were not accustomed to receiving tourists from Britain. An airline, claiming they wanted to re-build confidence in the Lebanon, had opened a twice-weekly route between Heathrow and Beirut, which is why I was able to get a flight.

I found a Beirut hotel by asking the aircrew, who gave me a lift to where they were staying. The following day I asked the hotel staff where I could ski, and armed with their suggestion, went out on to the streets to flag down a taxi. It had no windows in it except a windscreen, but undeterred, I gave the driver instructions, and set off on what I now think was one of the most dangerous journeys I have made, taking a Beirut taxi at that time

It was not like England, where once I entered a taxi it was my taxi exclusively for the duration of the ride. Over there, if someone else waved the taxi-driver down, they got in. One minute I was sitting in a taxi on my own, the next minute other men, absolute strangers, intent on going in roughly the same direction, joined me! The taxi had no lights and a cracked windscreen. It went down one-way streets the wrong way and stopped at frequent Shiite roadblocks.

I was driven in this manner up to a ski resort that had a couple of ski lifts and which, compared with the city of Beirut, was in a reasonable state. It was a small village quite up to Western standards as a modest intermediate resort, which surprised me. Other people were there skiing, and it was hot enough to lose skin layers in the sun.

The quality of the skiing, though, whatever that Australian's opinion, was awful. It was not extensive enough, and did not justify the trip. But the local operators, keen for me to go back to England with a good impression and spread the word, allowed me to ski over the top of the mountains where the soldiers were and into the notorious Bekaa Valley. The ski operators asked me why the British Government had never allowed English people to go there for thirty years; I did not want to explain to them that no one had actually wanted to go. They said that they had seen a French diplomat come out of Beirut, but they had never seen a British diplomat. I was only there for the skiing, I said, and voiced no other opinions. I did not pick up on the politics.

One effect of that trip was that it made me more serious about skiing, especially after an encounter with the famous Polar explorer, Robert Swan.

Later that year, in May 1994, George Möller, Dutch chief executive of the London branch of the bank, Pierson Heldring Pierson (PHP), with whom we did business, invited me on an annual May walk called *Wadwalk* to the island of Ammeld on the Dutch coast. I thought it would be a simple five miles or so, and felt capable of doing it even though I was, at the time, overweight. It had been presented to me as a walk over sand dunes, and not especially arduous. I had not walked five miles for years, let alone, as George proposed, through the sea. Most of the time the water was ankle depth, but I discovered there were areas when I could be in up to my neck, and we all had poles to rescue ourselves with. There were occasions on these walks when people were unable to get across, because they had started when the tide was not low enough. Lots of people made the walk because it was quite fashionable, but there were people who were turned around and sent back.

I made it across.

By then the tide had risen, and we took a boat back. It was on that trip that I met another guest of the bank, Robert Swan. Robert told me later that he had noticed me because I was always out in front, always wanting to get on quicker than anyone else on the walk. He was also amused at hearing I had gone to Lebanon to ski. Early in the following year, Robert turned up at my office. He was looking for sponsors for an Antarctic expedition, and said he had been recommended to see me by another person in the City, in the process of cold-calling to raise sponsorship. It was hardly a cold call, though, because we all knew who he was; he had walked to the South Pole in 1986, and the North Pole in 1989/90, to become the first man ever to walk to both Poles.

Robert wanted to raise money to back a five-year programme between 1996 and 2001 called "Mission Antarctica", to clean up a Russian Antarctic base called Bellinghausen. The mission was focussed on 35 young people from 25 nations, involving them in the clean-up project, and was to be presented to the UN-backed World "Earth Summit" in Johannesburg in September 2002. Robert was accustomed to raising large amounts of sponsorship; the walk to the South Pole, "In the Footsteps of Scott", in 1985/6 had cost $8.4 million, and the North Pole "Icewalk" $11.2 million. "Project Antarctica", which had already cost $9.0 million when Robert contacted me, aimed to remove 1,000 tons of rubbish, an unsightly eye-sore in the pristine environment of Antarctica, taking it first to Ushuaia on the southern tip of Argentina, and then to a recycling plant in Uruguay. Costs included a large yacht to be called "2041" which it was planned to sail from Bellinghausen to South Africa, and be transported overland to be shown to the World Summit delegates in Johannesburg.

I found Robert Swan infectious, a can-do person with an enthusiasm for achieving things. He was inspirational and I wanted to support someone like him, doing what he did. But of course, part of me really wanted to be an active player rather than a passive backer. I knew I was not going to be such a player right then, because Robert was much fitter than me. I did offer a modest financial contribution to his efforts, but I also offered him my time. Even though I was chief executive of my own business, I offered three weeks of being a gofer to do anything he asked me to do.

He said he wanted to plan an Antarctic trip for the winter 1996/97 to celebrate the 60th Anniversary of the founding of UNICEF, involving children across the world. There were preparations to be made during the winter of 1995/96, and I offered to go and do whatever he needed me to do in southern Chile.

He asked me if I was serious. I said I was.

"Well," he said, "if you are going to do that, then you had better come on to Antarctica".

I said, "Fine". Naturally, I was delighted with the invitation.

A few months later he said, "Look, if you're coming on to Antarctica, do you want me to organise you getting to the South Pole?"

I said, "OK, then". Even better, going to the South Pole in the company of Robert Swan!

He said, "We are going in November".

In September, he and I bought all my clothes to go to the South Pole, and I bought my ticket. I was not going to be doing very much, not going to walk anywhere, and the only travelling would be by aeroplane. But I was not *trying* to be a tourist. At that time, all I wanted to be was a gofer. If I had thought it was just about going to the South Pole as a tourist I would not have gone. Because I was with Robert, I wanted to learn, and to be part of something big that he was putting together.

Unfortunately his sponsor, AT&T, announced a demerger and he lost his sponsorship money. He came back to me and said he was no longer going in November. I had a choice to make. Having paid for my flights, did I go ahead on my own to the South Pole, without Robert? Or did I just try and get a refund? The deciding factor was that I had, after all, told a lot of people I was going to Antarctica, so I opted to go. I flew down to Punta Arenas in Chile, and then on to the Antarctica base camp on my own, meeting other people doing the same thing. From base camp, called Patriot Hills, I was flown into the South Pole.

I looked around and then was flown out again.

Most people arriving at Patriot Hills used the base camp for climbing Mount Vinson, Antarctica's highest Mountain, with a small number of other expeditions walking to the South Pole. But while I was there a Canadian called Bill Arras set out to become the first person to pilot a hot air balloon in Antarctica. The only other hot air balloon had been used by Captain Scott in 1902, but Scott had always tethered it to the ground and used it as a look out post. When I realised there was room in Bill Arras's balloon for two people, I offered Bill a modest sponsorship to put my company name on his basket. He accepted the money, but not my request to join his short flight, saying I did not have the appropriate insurance.

The only activity I had been able to do was a modest amount of cross-country skiing around Patriot Hills, but even that was limited because I was not insured for such activities, only for being a passenger. It was not anything like I had intended it to be. Instead of a useful journey making preparations for a serious explorer, I was a bystander watching other people do things. But it did give me a view of the topography of the Antarctic, and introduce me to a whole set of interesting people including the base camp staff. It was there that I met Mike Sharp, who turned out to be the key that opened the Antarctic to me.

Mike was an Englishman from Sheffield in Yorkshire, in his forties, and with the experience of having worked for the British Antarctic Survey, he was obviously familiar with Polar conditions. He was hard-working, demonstrated alone in the extraordinary amount of effort needed to keep the runway open at Patriot Hills to take in aircraft. Mike was out on the ice for very long hours every day in extremely cold conditions to make things work. He was employed by a company called Adventure Network International – ANI – that had arranged all my flights into and out of the Antarctic. Anne Kershaw, wife of Giles Kershaw, who had been killed in a gyrocopter accident in 1990 in Antarctica, ran this company.

The other significant person I met on that brief visit to Antarctica was Geoff Somers, who also worked for ANI. I collected business cards from both Mike and Geoff.

There was something captivating about Antarctica. It was so different from the way I had spent my life. There was the enormity of it, the white beauty, the open space and the mountains. There was nothing about it that I found unattractive. It was a solitary experience, a feeling of falling in love. Anyone fortunate enough to experience the interior of Antarctica, not on the coastline – I did not know the coastline – could not fail to love the wonder of the place. A lot of people who went there just keep going back and back and back, and I could see why they did. At that time of the year, with twenty-four hours of daylight, it was clean and dry. I thought it was wonderful.

I looked at all the different expeditions, including a band of Koreans climbing Mount Vinson, and knew I wanted to go back there one day, but on much different terms. It felt like another planet. I was looking in from the outside; next time I went back I wanted to be doing an expedition myself. At the time I was 42 years old, and in no physical condition to do any sort of serious walking. I did, though, make a private commitment that took years to realise. Meanwhile I had a living to make in the City of London, and I went back to making it.

But I dreamed.

In 1997, two years after that visit, Anne Kershaw asked me if I would like to be part of an expedition to ski across Greenland. She was a professional organiser of such expeditions, and I was expected to pay her to put it together and be part of it. She suggested we used dogs to pull sledges over the Greenland ice cap, with Innuit dog-drivers, and I would ski alongside the sledges. The expedition did not come off because two or three other people were going to be involved and then dropped out, and at that time I could not myself make the commitment. It weighed on me that I did not think I was fit enough to complete the journey. But the idea remained attractive, and was something for me to aim for, to justify the exercise I needed to do get fit again. I told Anne I could not do it, but would let her know in a year's time if she was still intending to organise such an expedition. From that point I started training, gym work and running, several times a week.

I wanted to get fit, to be able to ski a few hundred miles, but I did not want to make a big thing of it. Until then I had only been a recreational downhill skier. What I was planning was completely different from any skiing experience I had had so far. I wanted to learn cross-country skiing.

It was the appeal of being alone on the ice, dependent on my own skills to progress and survive, that drove me on. I said to myself, this is something I can do, and I want to do it. Once I signed off with myself that I was going to do it, the rest of it was actually hard physical work, but mentally it was easy. I said, this will only happen if I make it happen. All I had to do was go through the process of achieving it. As was often the case with me, I told some people about it before I even started training, and that way, I was not allowed to back out. But I did not tell everybody, only people before whom I would have been embarrassed to lose face.

I told Anne I would be ready to make such a trip over Greenland in the spring of 1999. That gave me a target to work towards.

At this time I commissioned a coat of arms. I did so because I am a traditionalist and felt I had made my own mark in life, and wanted to signal that fact, if only to myself. I enjoyed getting the genealogy of the family together. The Burtons are a family of peasants and agricultural workers, originally from Suffolk. I knew my strengths from my parents, that they came from a solid family background, and I wanted to get the genealogy up in the galleried hall at home, to show my children where we came from. They were the first generation in my family to look forward to a university education.

*Strong winds in Greenland required facial protection.*

Our Greenland destination, Dye 2, a relic of the Cold War, a DEW station abandoned in 1988.

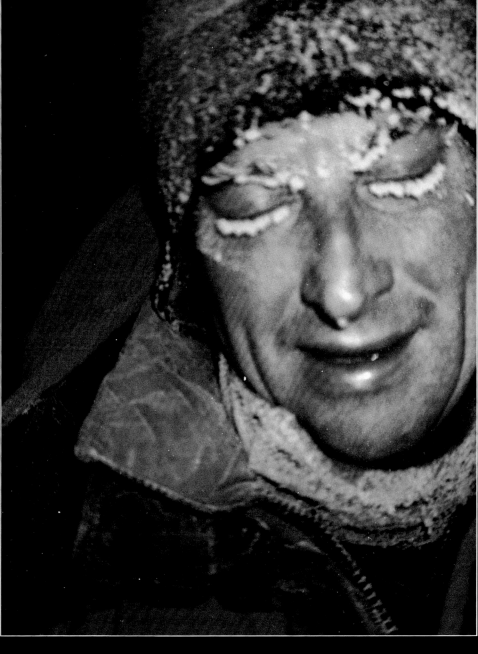

*First day on Russian training in Norilsk, too many clothes, too much perspiration.*

*Last day of Russian training, skiing in 23 hours of darkness.*

CONGRATULATIONS!
YOU ARE NOW AT

UHURU PEAK, TANZANIA, 5895M. AMSL.

AFRICA'S HIGHEST POINT
WORLD'S HIGHEST FREE-STANDING MOU

ONE OF WORLD'S LARGEST VOLCANOES.
WELCOME

*Mixing with the Polar elite in Norway.*

*Marek Kaminski*
*Poland*

*Martin Burton*

*Borge Ousland*          *Dr Mikhail ("Misha") Makalov*          *Mitsuro Olibo*
*Norway*                          *Russia*                                      *Japan*

*Training in Finse, Norway.*

*In the mountains between Finse and Outaoset.*

A coat of arms is meant to illustrate who you are, even who you think you are, which shows up in the design. Because I had promised myself I was going to make this trek, I wanted the coat of arms to reflect Antarctica. I felt that having done so, there was no way that I could back out of making the journey. The arms were, in effect, a contract with myself. I boxed myself in, deliberately. Even if a perfectly sensible reason came along to call the trip off, I could not take it. By having a penguin on the coat of arms, I was laying down a marker. In my own mind I had to be responsible to that marker.

As for the motto, I wanted "I don't regret", in the sense that "I don't wish to have regrets". I did not want to look back in retirement and wish I had done something that had been open for me to do, but which I had not done. I felt that, if a chance came to do something, I must do it before I was too old to do it. A lot of people do not pick up on opportunities in life, or make excuses about why they did not do something. (I hated the thought of looking back and saying I wish I had done something, when I could have done it, and I did not do it.) It was, I thought, an appropriate motto.

However, when the College of Arms came up with the Latin for what I requested, *Nil Factum Paenitendum*, I checked it with the distinguished economist and Latin scholar, Stephen Lewis, working in Monument Securities. Stephen told me that the College's interpretation "I do not regret" in Latin meant, in effect, that I had no conscience, that, for example, I could run over anyone and have no regrets about it. Clearly, this was not what I wanted. Stephen thought that the best way in Latin to express what I wanted to say was to turn it around to "Embrace the Opportunities". In Latin this is *Occasionem Amplectere*.

It was a personal thing. It was not something you inherited (well, some do, but coming from my background I did not inherit a coat of arms) and the one I had designed was personal to me. As I did not have any sons, the coat of arms was not something I could directly pass on either. I intended to put the arms on the back of my sledge; that created real problems later when the choice came to abandon the sledge, because I could not transfer the coat of arms to a new sledge.

But it was deeper than that.

23

I believed that if I did a big adventure with sledges, I needed to bring back the original sledge with the original coat of arms, much like a battle honour won on the field of arms.

# 3

# A Russian Test

To prepare for the possibility of Anne Kershaw's Greenland expedition, and because of my tenuous involvement with "Mission Antarctica", I had been invited to do some winter training in Russia, on the tundra near Norilsk, 2,000 miles northeast of Moscow. My guide, suggested by Robert Swan, was to be Dr Mikhail Makalov, known as Misha, a professional eye-surgeon but also a very experienced Polar traveller. He had done fifteen expeditions in the Arctic, including an amazing unsupported walk to the North Pole from Canada, and back again in 1994, with 123 days on the ice. Misha was involved with Robert's Bellinghausen clean-up operation, and prompted by Robert had offered to teach me how to survive in extremely cold temperatures. He would, of course, be paid for the job.

At this time, 1997/8, the Russians, organised by Robert Swan, were supplying a lot of the hardware and the manual labour for "Mission Antarctica", with funding coming from Western companies and individuals. Misha was keen to use the Bellinghausen clean-up operation as a symbolic gesture to the Russian Government, in effect saying that if Russia can clear up a station in

Antarctica, it should start clearing up some of the Arctic bases in Russia itself. We were all aware of the perilous situation that existed with the rotting submarines in the northern Russian port of Murmansk.

Misha also saw "Mission Antarctica" as an embarrassment to the West. If Russia could clear up its station in Antarctica, then why could the Western governments not clean up their own stations? They were certainly in need of being cleaned up. "Mission Antarctica" was a powerful symbolic gesture. It was not just the cleaning of one scientific station in Antarctica, but also young people showing the world, focussed on the Johannesburg "Earth Summit", what could actually be done.

Misha came to London first and inspected my kit, gear which Robert had helped me buy and which I had already used in Antarctica. Despite Robert's opinions, Misha refused to accept a lot of my clothing, and insisted I add to my wardrobe. He was pedantic about everything. Before the training started in December 1998, we went to his house in Ryazan, an old military town about 200 miles out of Moscow. Again, we did a little bit of training, an afternoon of cross-country skiing. His main purpose in getting me to visit Ryazan seemed to be so he could inspect my kit again, and again, he insisted I leave a sizable proportion behind.

Robert had referred to Misha as the "Mad Russian" who got him to the North Pole; apparently he was as hard as nails and did not feel the cold. Borge Ousland, probably the number one explorer in the world today, had sought advice from Misha. I felt I was lucky to get him to train me, as a peer beyond peers.

For the Polar training itself we flew four hours north to Norilsk, a hair-raising experience in a Russian airliner. We stayed in a rented apartment which we paid in American dollars. It belonged to a teacher who had not been paid for six months. He said he was happy going to work and not being paid, and hoping he was going to get half pay in a few months time. That far north in Russia was where Stalin had killed a million people. For a long time it had been closed to visitors. It had only been an open city since 1996, five years after the rest of Russia began to open up. When I arrived at the airport, police came and took my passport away. They were still suspicious of foreigners, and held us for a while at the airport. Although eventually I retrieved my passport, I would not have got it back as easily if I had been on my own, and was grateful Misha was able to get it for me.

Because Misha did not feel the cold, Robert had told me that I must take trousers made of down with me, and insist on bringing them, even though Misha would not want me to take them. Every time Misha said no, I was told to say yes. You will need them, said Robert, and he won't. Sure enough, at every level of inspection of the kit, Misha always said, "What are these?" I explained, patiently, what they were and why I wanted them. Because I was insistent, he had allowed them to get as far as the rented apartment in Norilsk.

Once again, though, he got out my equipment and went through it, and again started to query what I was taking. Because we had to pull it and carry it, he said, he had to ensure that we did not have anything excessive. I had a down jacket, and he asked me why I was taking it? The straight answer was that the down jacket had kept me warm in Antarctica when it was minus thirty-three degrees at the South Pole. I knew how good my down jacket was, and we were facing conditions in northern Russia of minus 40 and near on 24 hours of darkness.

I could not believe he was telling me that I did not need it.

He said, if you insist, we would take one down jacket between us, but I could see he did not believe we should even do that.

Then he said, "What are these?"

"I've told you," I said, "They are down trousers"

"You don't need them. When are you going to wear them?"

"I don't know," I said, irritably, "I just know that Robert said I must take them even though you're going to tell me I don't need them. I haven't got a reason or justification, I'm just saying to you that Robert told me I must insist."

Misha was put out. He sat cross-legged in the middle of the room, adamant that he was right. It was obvious that he was accustomed to getting his own way. The idea that we were going to be carrying down trousers on this journey because I thought I needed them to keep me warm did not appeal to him at all.

"We're going out now," he said, getting up. "Wear what you want. We're going to do some training, but we're going to come back here afterwards, we're going to stay one more night in the apartment."

He started making preparations to leave. When I looked outside it was still minus forty degrees, so I duly put on my down jacket because I needed it, and we set off. We drove to the outskirts of the town, and did only two hours of skiing. At the end I was sweating like a pig. Every piece of clothing on me was drenched with sweat. When we got back to the apartment Misha told me the clothes I was wearing were now useless.

"We won't even have time to dry them on the radiator," he said, "and obviously when we are out there we will have no radiator. So you can see that you do not need them. You will generate your own heat."

In this way, he taught me that I did not have to go out with my down jacket, however cold the temperature. When we set off on our training I did not have the choice of wearing the jacket, because it was soaking wet. But we did take his down jacket. He made this one concession in case I became ill. He did not want to take the down trousers either, but he allowed me to take them.

On the first night we made camp, the temperature was 40 below, centigrade. I got into my sleeping bag, proof against a temperature of minus 45 degrees, a bag that had worked wonderfully well in the Antarctic summer. It did not work in the Arctic winter. The difference between the two was that in the Antarctic there had been twenty-four hours of sunlight coming through the tent, creating warmth. In the dark Arctic night I had no such comfort. I put on more layers of clothes inside the sleeping bag to retain my warmth, and found I had run out of clothes.

Misha asked me how I was feeling.

"I'm OK," I said, obviously not OK, "but I'm just not warm enough to go to sleep."

I told him I had to keep moving in the sleeping bag.

"Why don't you wear your down trousers?" he asked.

I had never dreamt I would wear my down trousers in the sleeping bag, but sure enough I wore them on top of my gear and then I was warm enough to go to sleep. I felt Robert did well telling me I needed my down trousers, even if I did not know where I was going to use them. That is where I used them, in the sleeping bag. Misha made no comment about his opposition to my taking them.

He was able to sleep under lighter covering than me. Russians are accustomed to the cold. I did not sleep in my down trousers every night, but certainly that first night it made a big difference.

I learnt that it was not the cold that kills in such freezing temperatures, because I could do something about the cold. To get too hot could kill me. I must never let my clothes get wet with sweat, there was no place on expeditions to dry them out. Misha trained me never to allow my clothes to get wet. And the only way to avoid that happening was to wear less clothing and to ensure I had total ventilation. Eventually all I was wearing was a 100-fleece shirt, and a wind-proof jacket, releasing zips on the wind-proof jacket all the way up, under the arms, all the way down, leaving them to flap. My entire blue fleece went into white hoarfrost as I sweated; the sweat came through the fleece and froze. I learned that my working temperature should be always just below comfortable, that I had to keep working, and that enabled me to survive. As soon as I stopped working, I had to take a hard brush and quickly brush off the hoarfrost, then stick my fleeces on. Of course, by that time, I was no longer sweating.

I ate a lot, much of it fat. Nuts did not freeze, so they were a staple diet. Chocolate was difficult to eat, but it was a good short-term substitute. In Russia we ate a lot of boiled bacon fat. It was not quite bacon, but it was meat without much lean on it.

Every morning when we broke camp and we were standing around pulling down the tent, we half-froze wearing virtually nothing. Misha had a catch phrase he was always using: "Only hard work will save us now." It then took twenty minutes' hard work to generate enough heat to keep warm.

I learned tent procedures from Misha, making sure, for example, my sleeping bag never came inside the tent when I was not using it, or when I was cooking. The bag could only come inside when all the cookers were off. If the stove was on, anything made from down had to be outside the tent, otherwise it would absorb the warm moisture in the air. Cooking created warmth, which created dampness, and if I had a damp sleeping bag I had a problem. I have since heard other people, far more experienced than me, ask if I suffered from damp sleeping bags. I was able to tell them I had not suffered because of lessons I learned from Misha; I also learned to tie the bag to tent poles outside so it did not blow away.

I spent a week on the Russian tundra. It was one to one, the wise man passing knowledge to the tyro. I got on very well with Misha; we are still friends today. We became friends despite the fact that our relationship started as a commercial deal, me paying him to pass on his knowledge.

We did not travel big distances, averaging about ten kilometres a day entirely by skiing, without the aid of kite or sail. The point of the trip was not about going from one place to another; but about the technique that you get there, setting up camp, breaking it down in the morning. After seven days Misha claimed to be satisfied with what I had learned.

Inside the tent, much of our conversation was about the perceptions of Russians about the English, and perceptions of the English about Russia. I felt at the end of it, that I had the mental confidence to deal with the Greenland trip.

He said, "After this I don't know why you're doing the Greenland trip, Greenland is going to be easy compared to this".

But I needed the confidence to know. I had been taught how to survive, now I wanted to use the skills I had been taught. This included skiing by torchlight, which we did in such extreme conditions in Russia. I would not meet worse conditions in either Greenland or in the summer months of the Antarctic.

At the end of the trip we bumped into a hunter on a primitive 1960s skidoo. It was a shock to this man, in what had been a highly restricted area, to see two people skiing, one of them a foreigner! Misha told him what we were doing, and gave him a date when we were coming out of the tundra and arriving back on the edge of the city. He obviously passed this news on. When we arrived back at Norilsk there was a television crew waiting to receive us and whisk us off to the TV studios. They interviewed both of us. Misha was already a hero in Russia, one of the three hundred Heroes of the Soviet Union, and the only non-military official hero. The mere fact that he was in Norilsk was big news. They wanted to know what he was doing, what I was doing, and was this a trend? Perhaps there would be commercial opportunities for tourism?

I came back from Russia in December 1998, having acquired an odd habit that lasted until I gave up smoking cigars years later. Whenever I bought a box of matches, I kept one match sticking out of the end. This came from having freezing hands; it is then possible for numbed hands to grasp it.

I felt ready to tackle Greenland as the next learning stage for my return trip to Antarctica, this time for real.

# 4

# Greenland with Dogs

Anne Kershaw had suggested the Greenland journey in 1997. She had wanted me to help fund such a journey with others, but I had not felt physically fit enough then to do it. It was, though, a real goal to aim at and I decided to do it independently of Anne two years later. I started training three times a week. There were two options in Greenland. One was to do a complete crossing, east to west, over the ice cap, which went up to 9,000 feet. The other was to walk from the east coast to Dye 2, the DEW-line station that had been abandoned in 1988, in the middle west of Greenland. The Dye 2 journey was 350 kilometres, the complete crossing 500 kilometres. Because I could devote only a limited amount of time to the trip, I focussed on the shorter one to Dye 2.

I had to allow at least three weeks to do the actual journey, skiing alongside a dog sled driven by a Greenland Innuit. I also had to allow a week either side for getting in to eastern Greenland to prepare for the journey, and getting out afterwards. Taking five weeks off was about the most I could justify taking off work. The complete crossing of Greenland would take an extra two to three weeks on top of that, and although attractive I could not justify two months away from the City of London.

The Russian training had given me confidence in my own abilities, but I wanted to test these out. It was one thing to sit in an armchair and believe I could do something. It was another to actually do it. I also felt that I needed help in risking such a trip, which was outside my normal experience. With the little experience I had, it would not have been sensible to punt off on my own. If I needed rescuing in such circumstances, I would have been heavily criticised. It was, I thought, fitting that I took a staggered approach to the biggest of the adventures I had in mind. If I eventually wanted to make such a journey solo, I had to work up to it.

I remembered Mike Sharp, one of the base crew at Patriot Hills in Antarctica, and asked him if he would navigate for me, joining the trip as a professional guide. He agreed.

Conditions in Greenland were the opposite of those in Russia. On the dates I chose to go, there were twenty-four hours of daylight. We could not navigate by the stars, even presuming we had the skills to do so, because we could not see them. Like all modern Polar travellers, we used a GPS, a global positioning system.

The Greenland journey started in May 1999 when Mike Sharp and I flew into Kulusuk, a former DEW-line station on an island halfway up the east coast. We then travelled to Ammassalik, an Innuit village across the bay. Ammassalik was also an island, and with 1,400 people it was the biggest village on the whole east coast of Greenland. From there, we had to get to the mainland itself, and as the ice was beginning to break up, we aimed to do that by helicopter. There was a helicopter available locally that ferried food supplies to Isortoq, a much smaller village with 100 residents on the mainland.

We had found the dogs for the journey through an Italian called Peroni who had chosen to live in Greenland for the last twenty years. He arranged two dog teams for us, and the two Innuit dog drivers, Tobias Ignatiussen in charge of my sled, and Pedter Ignatiussen to drive for Mike. Curiously, only a small number of native Greenlanders have actually been on the ice cap, and neither dog team had gone into the interior before. It was usually foreigners who made such journeys.

Any Greenland Innuit who went up into the interior was considered a hero in his own village. There was a simple reason why it was so rare for locals. There was no food there; why go where there was no food, just to come back?

Locals also had an added fear of the wind, the fiercest of which was called *Piterak*. People on expeditions had died, literally been blown away, and those stories had passed down the generations and been exaggerated. Anyone who went up on the ice cap – in the villagers' eyes – was risking his life. The Danes, who governed Greenland, were selective as to who could travel across the ice cap. They licensed such journeys, and required proof of the correct equipment, with an inspection point at Ammassalik. We had to apply to get permits to make the journey, and the kit inspection was rigorous because the Danes did not want the trouble and expense of rescuing a half-baked expedition in the middle of Greenland. Our inspection was on May 2.

After that, we were delayed for six days by bad weather, and we could not actually reach Isortoq on the mainland. It was an extra worry to me that I had been doing a lot of running to get fit in the months up to that journey, and about three weeks earlier I had found myself suffering from shin splints. My legs hurt so badly I could hardly walk down the road to the shop. I could not believe I had been that unlucky, but having poured so much of my time into making this journey work, I could not call it off.

I rationalised with myself, saying that what was painful was putting my foot down on the ground, and with skiing my foot was already on the ground so I was only going to slide it. I felt that I could work through the pain and complete the journey, but decided I could not keep my injuries secret from Mike Sharp. He suggested I went down to the local hospital in the village of Ammassalik, and they gave me anti-inflammatory tablets. Because of the bad weather, I was able to take six day's rest, and with the combination of the enforced rest, the tablets, and creams I had already bought in Iceland, my legs improved. The shin splints went away as a major problem, and thankfully, did not come back. On the journey itself I was pleased that my reasoning was correct; the action of skiing was less stressful than walking.

We spent the six days waiting in a small wooden hotel in Ammassalik, which was comfortable and quite close to the airfield. On the seventh day the weather improved, we were ready to go, but we had a problem. The helicopter was only going to make one trip between Ammassalik and Isortoq, and there was not enough room to carry all of us. We needed to use dog teams domiciled at Ammassalik because they were well-fed, worked regularly and were looked after, and their drivers were experienced. The dog teams on the mainland in the village of Isortoq were in much poorer condition, being exercised less often, and getting less food, and consequently, their drivers were less experienced.

A risky solution was found, though it was not risky to Mike or me.

Some of us piled into the helicopter, me in front, Mike and my Innuit driver Tobias Ignatiussen in the back, with 14 dogs on Tobias's team sitting all over them, panting, and the sledge slung under the helicopter. Mike's driver, Peter Ignatiussen, was so keen to get the overland job that he set off across the breaking ice surface between Ammassalik and Isortoq, and drove his team of dogs and sledge over the 50 statute miles between the two villages. Some of this journey was over land, but most of it was over dangerous disintegrating sea ice. He and his dogs won through, and when we tested the quality of the Isortoq dogs teams – we gave two teams of them a day's work getting us established on the ice cap – we were grateful to have him.

Because we were running late we needed to push on quickly; there were flights booked from the other side of Greenland to take us home, but we had to get going fast to have any chance of catching them. The two dog teams were going to carry all our equipment, with the Innuit riding on their sledges and Mike and I skiing beside them. Having two sledges was a luxury and gave us the scope to carry whatever we wanted. Contrary to much I had been taught by Misha in Russia, if there was an opportunity to take two of something instead of one, we took it. We had a lot of resources, which helped with my confidence. If we did hit trouble, I thought we had the means to get ourselves out of it without calling for outside help.

Oddly, the Innuit suffered badly from the cold, because there was no hard physical work involved in sitting on sledges. They had to wear much more clothing than we wore. An early lesson, which I had not learned from Misha, was that the system of not wearing a lot of clothes only worked when it was not windy. Greenland was windy. We had to wear more clothing than we wanted when it was windy, and the wind remained a problem all the way across to Dye 2. By the time we reached the last day, I was glad it was the last day.

In all, we skied for eleven days, and averaged nearly thirty-two kilometres, about sixteen nautical miles, a day. The dogs did the hard physical work of pulling the sledges, and all Mike and I had to do was ski along side them. We had no other aids, such as kites and sails, which I was to have later in the Antarctic. At that time I did not know how to use either.

We split each day into four travelling periods, each period two hours long. We skied for two hours, stopped and rested, then skied for another two hours, and so on. It meant skiing at an average of four kilometres an hour, which was not very fast.

The dogs would have outrun us if they had been allowed to. They were strictly controlled and pulling a lot of weight, though, ironically, the weightiest load on the sledges was their food. One dog team had a peculiar foible; it could not lead the other dog team. In a whiteout, aiming into whiteness, one dog team could do it and the second dog team could not.

We also challenged the prevailing view about how dogs should be harnessed. In Greenland, it was normal to have a fan system of harnessing dogs on the trail, compared to places like Canada, where they harnessed dogs in pairs. The difference was to do with terrain. Canada is full of forests, with narrow trails, and fan harnessing would not work. Greenland Innuit, who had no trees and did have wide-open spaces, preferred the fan. But we found that on the ice cap, pairs worked better for leading. It meant only two dogs had to do the leading and all the others followed.

We also found we had only two dogs prepared to lead. They had a strong pecking order, and when either of the lead dogs got tired or was threatened with an injury, it was a problem knowing what to do about it.

I fed them once, a job normally done by their Innuit handlers. They were fed seal meat to begin with, and when that ran out they were fed dog biscuit. We gave them some of our own medicine, anti-inflammatory stuff, along with injections to keep them going. One dog was quite ill and we offered to fly it back, but the Innuit said no, and the dog rode on the sled for a while. Remarkably, when we finally arrived at our destination, the Innuit turned the dog teams around and set off to sledge back over the 350 kms we had just covered. All dogs returned safely to Ammassalik.

We had friendly relations with the Innuit, but they had only a few words of English and we could speak neither Innuit nor Danish. It was a relationship of nods and hands waving and pointing. We offered them our food but they wanted to eat seal meat with the dogs. They had their own ways of living.

The last day was difficult, closer to what I had wanted to experience than the other ten days. We had 40 kilometres left to do to reach Dye 2, a little longer than our average day's travel. A few days earlier we had bumped into three Danes using a kite, going from west to east, the opposite direction to us. They were aiming to be the first all-Danish team to cross Greenland, and it was my first experience of seeing a kite work. We told them we were going to Dye 2, because, we thought, it had been totally abandoned but our pick-up aircraft could land there. The Danes said there were two Americans there, training with Hercules aircraft and monitoring the weather.

"When you get there," they told us, "the Americans will give you two nice steaks."

That was a big temptation in my mind on what I saw as the last day, that at the end of it I was going to eat a steak. But when we broke camp the weather was poor. We set out anyway, but after five kilometres Mike asked if I thought we should stop? Because the weather was so bad, it had been particularly difficult to break camp, and I had formed the opinion that if we did not keep going, then we would not get there.

"Let's just keep going and we will get there," I told Mike. "There are forty kilometres to do, we have done five, we can do the other 35 if we just keep going."

I knew that Mike was a more experienced traveller than me, and yet I had voiced a strong opinion, apparently contradicting him. Why? It was because I believed he was checking to see if I wanted to go on. For him, perhaps it was obvious we should stop because of my inexperience. But I felt that all he was looking for was an expression of confidence that it was all right to keep going. I was calm about it.

The Innuit only had a say in the decision if they could not get their dogs to work. If we went, so did they.

It became extremely windy; including the wind-chill, we discovered later at Dye 2, temperatures dropped to minus 58. It was not just cold, but we experienced a number of whiteouts. Most of the trip we had been able to navigate by watching our shadows as the sun moved around the sky. In whiteout conditions there was no shadow. Another problem was that the two dog teams would not travel at the same speed. We could live with that in clear conditions, but in whiteout conditions we lost sight of each other. Mike skied alongside one dog team, I skied alongside the other. There were two or three occasions on that last day when we lost each other. We did not know where the other dog team was, and it was scary. I insisted on having a shovel so if we did get lost and could not continue, I could dig in and wait for better conditions. Mike had the navigation equipment, I did not, and nor did the Innuit. There was only one navigating sledge because I did not have a GPS.

I am not sure how we did not get lost completely. Mike and his Innuit would perhaps be only a hundred yards in front of us; we just did not know exactly where he was or if we were wandering off track. If something went wrong with our dogs, the danger was that Mike and his Innuit would draw away from us and then, where were they? We prayed there would not be a tangling of lines with the dogs when we were lost. If we kept going at the same speed, we hoped that when visibility improved we would catch up with them. That happened twice. My heart was in my mouth on at least those occasions. I really needed it to go right, because otherwise we were going to be digging a hole and seeing the weather out until the morning.

In that way, with five two-hour stints over eleven hours, we made it through to Dye 2, but even when the GPS told us we were there, we could not find it. We had been told we would see Dye 2 from forty miles away, but not that day. Then we ran across a flag in the ground. We walked on to find another flag, and eventually we came across a tent with two Americans in it. I was so happy to find them.

By this stage I was very cold (my feet took two months to recover), and in a warm marquee tent it took twenty minutes to undress. It would have been a real struggle to continue the journey in the condition we were in. It was a bad day, but we had gone for it despite the appalling weather, knowing it was our last day. The goal was to get those two steaks.

Unfortunately, both Americans were vegetarians.

We had a satellite phone with us and called for an aircraft to come and pick us up from Kangerlussuaq on the west coast of Greenland. An aircraft flew out of Sondestrum, the airport there, twice a week, via Kulusuk, to Iceland.

The crossing of Greenland was a personal triumph. I think the last day was within my capacity because of the training in Russia. If I had not had the Russian training I would not have had the mental capacity to complete the trip. I would have said, let's stop. But I was comfortable within myself, and felt I had been prepared. Everything, I felt then, whether crossing Greenland or trading the markets, was about preparation and making sure I had done it right. That last day worked because of the preparation.

On the human level, I struck up a good relationship with Mike Sharp. I liked him before the trip and I liked him afterwards. I did have one reservation. On our last night in Iceland after our trip had ended, bearing in mind I had covered his wages and all his costs, he didn't buy me a Guinness. Later that evening I raised the subject.

"Look, you're still treating me like a client," I said, "I think you owe me more than that."

He bought the next round.

When I mulled over the whole experience, I came to feel that Greenland was not as challenging as I had thought it would be. Not pulling my sledge just made it too easy. Dogs were allowed in the Arctic, but for environmental reasons, no longer allowed in the Antarctic. Down south, I would have to pull my own sledge.

The whole point about doing these trips was to get a mental challenge out of it. It was a challenge, not just in preparing the trip and getting it completed, because that was actually quite a lot of fun, but also conceiving an idea and making it happen. On the Greenland trip I was looking for something that really tested me, but mostly that did not happen. I wanted to come through the test on my own terms, but only the last day was a bit like that, because it was so difficult. I was pleased about that last day. There were not enough last days for me.

A factor in putting these journeys together was a concern that I would

*Patriot Hills as we arrive. Twin Otters have flown down the peninsula to prepare runway.*

*Ronny Finsaas, Martin Burton, Geoff Somers at Patriot Hills, Dec 3, 2003.*

*A dangerous time as the aircraft propeller is used to inflate the canopy, ahead of the first balloon flight in Antarctica (1995).*

*Mike Sharp and Martin Burton at Patriot Hills, ahead of leaving by air for the South Pole.*

*Thiel Mountains – first Twin Otter flight of the 2003 season to the Pole requires digging out fuel drums from the previous season.* © Ronny Finsaas

*Martin Burton at Geographic South Pole (just right of US flag).*

*Ready to go, the wind is almost perfect.*

become too old before I had done all the difficult journeys I dreamed of. Antarctica was still in my mind, and Greenland was a stepping-stone, but it had not been as big a stepping-stone as I had thought it was going to be.

In any case I came back to London and got fat.

I did not do anything for two years, but frequented a fine selection of restaurants. Without an immediate goal I found it difficult to maintain a regime of fitness. I did not keep fit, and let myself go.

It took until the summer of 2001 for me to realise I had to do something. It could, I thought, be *anything*, but I had to do something.

With the realisation came the sobering thought that, to be prepared for a serious journey, I needed another two or three years to get into condition. This was not just physical condition, but the whole business of putting a journey together. In three years time I would be fifty years of age. That meant I had to start immediately, and 2001 was the last chance to set the whole thing rolling.

But what was I to do in the Antarctic? There had to be a genuine goal.

After some thought, I recalled that I had met a man called Roger Mears in Antarctica in 1995. He had determined to start walking from Hercules Inlet, the nearest coastline to the South Pole, and pulling his sledge to cross the whole continent via the Pole, solo and unsupported. He set out to do this but had to give up because, he claimed, of the bad design on his sledge. He had put the sledge on stilts in order for it to glide over the snow better, but in the wrong type of snow it just sank into it. He told me that the sledge was difficult to pull out and change direction. He tried for forty-four days and then gave up.

He had only got halfway to the Pole, but more importantly, he told me that there was a psychological barrier at forty days. Beyond that, he said, every-thing got worse.

Could I make a similar journey from the Pole to Hercules Inlet?

I accepted that the forty-day barrier that Mears ran into was because he walked solo. But it had not been the psychological barrier that had stopped him, but his sledge. I thought the forty-day barrier was an interesting challenge. I did not have to do it on my own, as I was still an amateur. But what would it be like to do 40 days on an expedition?

I asked Robert Swan if there was anything he would like to do in Antarctica, the inference being that I would support such an expedition. I said that I did not care if we went around in circles, but I wanted to be on the Antarctic ice for forty days.

"Is there a trip that you want to do that fits those limits?" I asked him

He told me there was, because of the failure he had felt in 1996, when he was not able to complete his journey, made with Geoff Somers and Crispin Day, to be the first men to ski sail from the South Pole to Hercules Inlet, the nearest sea coast to the Pole. Robert had actually set off on that journey with Somers and Day, to commemorate the sixtieth anniversary of the founding of UNICEF, but his UNICEF commitments in Argentina meant he felt he had to pull out halfway through, being air-lifted off at Thiel Mountains. Somers and Day had completed the journey on their own, and were the first to do it.

Perhaps, he said, we could go back and complete it? Start from the South Pole and do the whole thing again?

"That's the sort of thing I had in mind," I said, full of enthusiasm.

"That would fit into your plan, would it?" he asked. I said it would, but I wanted a second travelling companion.

"What about Misha. Would he want to come?"

Robert thought he would.

Fantastic!

The idea that I would do a serious Antarctic trip with Misha, the "peer beyond peers" whom I had learned to respect for his toughness and his Arctic skills, and with Robert Swan, was to me the ultimate adventure.

I needed such an adventure as an inspiration.

In those two years I had grown to be the best part of eighteen stone – 250 pounds – and I started my training by taking a video of myself, in all my overweight glory.

I told the camera what I wanted to be doing on my fiftieth birthday.

The camera still reminds me of the physical state I started from.

# 5

# Kilimanjaro and Altitude Training

When I had approached Robert Swan in the summer of 2001 to share an adventure together, he said it should happen in the winter of 2003/4. That was two and a half years away. To fulfil my side of the bargain I would have to make a decision to commit by March 2002. That meant reducing my weight from eighteen stone, losing about 40 pounds to get close to fifteen stone. I would also have to start paying out money for the project as it unfolded.

Robert suggested that, come March 2002 I should employ a fellow traveller friend of his, Crispin Day to start buying up-to-date equipment, including kites and sails. Day would require payment for this job. Then I needed to get acclimatised to altitude, because the South Pole was 9,400 feet above sea level, though it felt higher because of the dryness and the cold, an effect of being over 12,000 feet. As many people suffered altitude sickness at the Pole, I was curious to see how I would cope. To do this, I decided I should climb the highest mountain in Africa, Kilimanjaro.

Nothing turned out quite as planned. The first blow came nine months after outlining the project with Robert Swan. I went to see him and told him I had made good progress.

"I am on the way to being fit," I said, "And I am committed to spending forty days on the ice."

But Robert now felt differently. He felt he could not commit to the journey. The big project he had been involved in, "Mission Antarctica", had taken a lot more money than he had anticipated. Things had gone wrong with the ship that he had been involved with, and he could not afford to take two to three months out on an expedition. The project we had planned together would not have made him money. It might have assisted his CV, and been included in his talks, but it would not pay his bills. He felt he must continue to work, lecturing and rebuilding his financial resources.

He said he thought it much better that he told me now than later.

This was a disappointment. I had been excited by the thought of sharing a trip with someone as distinguished as Robert Swan. Working as a trader for many years, disappointments were commonplace, so I shrugged off my feelings. It was the only way to cope. If it went wrong today, then it could go right tomorrow. None of the backing I had given to Robert's expedition had bought loyalty, as the money was not given for those reasons. I still had Misha as a prospective travelling companion, and if Robert was not going to be with us, that was reality. I had to move on, and I did so.

Robert turned me down in the spring of 2002, but felt sure that Misha would continue. I outlined the forty-day idea in detail to Misha. He found it interesting, and said he would do it. I put it to him that I needed altitude training and intended to climb Kilimanjaro, to see how altitude affected me. Would he like to come as my guest? It was not going to be a sponsored corporate event. It would just be the two of us, and whatever local guides we needed. I told him I would cover his expenses, and he agreed to come.

A guide was necessary, as was a cook and a number of bearers. We planned to start the climb in Tanzania, and the authorities there organised this for me. I wanted to use the climb to bond with Misha again, and to plan the Antarctica trip at the end of the following year. Misha arrived in London from Russia in September 2002. We flew into Tanzania via Nairobi and then Arusha, and immediately ran into a problem which angered me.

Ten days before our climb, three bearers on another expedition had died from exposure on the mountain. The way the system worked in Tanzania was we booked our guide and cook through the local agency, who selected from sixty to seventy licensed guides. These guides then went to the gates of the compound where the climb started, and picked from people queuing up to get a job as a bearer. None of the bearers had any special clothing as protection against the elements, so they were ill-equipped to climb a mountain. There were certain times of the year, such as the rainy season, when you would not want to climb Kilimanjaro. If the weather changed unexpectedly, as it had done ten days earlier with heavy rain, the native bearers did not have adequate equipment to protect themselves from the weather. Some of them died of exposure, yet this was deemed an acceptable risk. The bearers who would be climbing with us were carrying heavy loads while we were carrying backpacks. They too had inadequate protection.

This offended me. Safety was always foremost in my mind. The risk of loss of life just so I could test myself for altitude sickness upset me. I didn't like it at all and resolved to do what I could about it when I returned to the office in Arusha.

There were four routes to climb up Kilimanjaro. We did not take the hardest route or the easiest route either. We walked through forestation to begin with, and when we got to around 11,000 feet, I still felt fine. I had slight fuzziness, but I was OK. It was a six-day trip, and I became confident I was coping. In terms of physical exercise I felt it was quite easy, though this was an illusion. As a result of over-confidence I used up too much energy on day 5 after a steep part of the climb, and ended with a severe headache. I was rattling with pills, could not sleep, and we were not carrying oxygen.

I felt very ill.

It was customary to tip the people helping us at the end of the expedition, but I decided the day before going for the summit that I wanted them to know they would get their money whether I made it to the top or not. There were set rules about how much they should receive, a daily rate, and how much to be tipped. The guide, on $10/day, was best paid. The cook got $5/day, and the bearers $3/day. The same ranking was supposed to apply to tips. I had asked what the normal tip was and heard that the bearers expected to receive $10/15.

Both the guide and the cook had all-weather gear, I knew I wanted to help bearers to buy the means to improve their chances of survival, but I could not do so without adding to the money I had to pay both the guide and the cook. I gave the guide $75 instead of his normal $50, at which he was very pleased, as was the cook, to whom I gave $60 instead of $30. I then told the bearers I was paying them extra because I expected them to buy some clothes so they did not run the risk of dying of exposure on the mountain next time around.

When the guide and the cook saw the seven bearers dancing on the mountain waving their $50 tips, their mood changed from delight to fury. The guide came back to me and demanded more money. He wanted his differentials. If the bearers got $50, he said, he should certainly get a lot more, even though he had received much more than he had expected. Because he claimed I had not got the ranking right, he had a problem. I endeavoured to explain to him why I thought the bearers should have a large tip, to enable them to buy the equipment that would keep them alive, and there were lots of second hand clothes at the bottom of the mountain that they could buy. This did not satisfy him.

Meanwhile, Misha, as a doctor, was doing his bit to alleviate the bearers' plight, giving those balancing large loads on their necks and heads painkillers and other medicines.

On the penultimate day we left at 8 am, and finished at 1pm. The idea was to rest through to midnight, then start climbing for the summit. The guide allowed us seven hours to get to the top and then return back, dropping to 13,000 feet. We were to climb from 15,000 feet to 19,340 feet in those seven hours, stand at the top and then turn back down again, descending 6,000 feet, in the same day.

There was nothing technically difficult about the climb, and it was, in fact, more of a walk. I watched the terrain change, first forest, then practically a desert and then it became shingle and ice cap. Nothing grew at the top, above 18,000 feet.

Despite feeling ill I made it to the summit of Kilimanjaro, as of course, did Misha.who felt 100 per cent.

We took photographs and stayed on the summit for half an hour, with me nursing a severe headache. I felt terrible I just needed sleep. We dropped down about 1,500 feet quickly. It was steep at the top, but after that quick descent, I stopped.

"Can I go to sleep now?" I asked.

I perched myself on a rock and immediately fell asleep. When I woke I asked Misha how long I had been out. "Only about fifteen minutes," he said. I felt so much better for the nap. I had not slept in forty eight hours previously, suffering from the altitude. We continued down the mountain, the weather remained benign and there was no immediate threat to the bearers.

It is more common to get injured on the way down a mountain, and that was especially true on the last day before getting back to base. I damaged my toes from the pressure of my boots from the continual descent.

On the last day, making camp, an African came up to us after a six-hour climb from below. He was carrying a case of beer. Nothing could have been more welcome! He had paid half a dollar a bottle for the beer, but sold it to us at two dollars. For $18 on the deal, he was lucky we were not teetotallers, but I really appreciated his entrepreneurial spirit.

It was the first time I had ever climbed a serious mountain, and part of me felt moderately pleased. But fifteen thousand people a year climb Kilimanjaro, so it is very achievable. I was happy that I had got to 15,000 feet without being incapacitated by the altitude, and that I could even cope at 19,000 feet, albeit with difficulty. As 14,000 feet was the virtual height of the South Pole, I felt that I had achieved what I wanted.

I complained to the agency about the lack of safety measures taken by them to look after the lives of the bearers. I think Westerners, people who travel to climb Kilimanjaro, must insist that suitable clothing is provided for bearers. We were not allowed under Tanzanian law to employ our own bearers, because the authorities claimed the current system gave work to the tribes at the bottom of the mountain. But if the official Tanzanian agency knew that we were going to hire seven bearers, they should have turned up with seven rucksacks and seven capes. We should, as a matter of decency, insist that people we hire at the gate are well clothed. Sponsoring a trip, charity or not, if I had had one of my bearers die on me, I would not have felt good about it at all.

One of our problems in insisting on a higher standard from these agencies was that we felt politically incorrect in making such demands. The overwhelming majority of Tanzanians were African and Christian, and a tiny minority were Muslim and of Indian origin. The Muslims appeared to be earning the money and not looking after the Africans. All the people with the brains in Arusha, the people with Toyota trucks, the bright ones, were not of African origin.

Tanzania was one of the poorest countries I had been to. I did not like going there feeling I was exploiting them, but I felt we did.

Misha, my Russian friend will be a worthy companion for an Antarctic trek.

I did not know then the bizarre way I was going to lose him as a partner.

# 6

# Norway

When Robert Falcon Scott – Scott of the Antarctic – trekked to the South Pole in 1912, he and his doomed team of four companions man-hauled their sledges most of the way there and back. If they were lucky, they averaged ten miles a day. Modern techniques of Antarctic travel involve using sails and kites to haul both skier and sledge, capable in some cases of generating speeds of more than 30 mph. I had no experience of using either kite or sail, and there was one obvious place to learn, in Norway.

Misha was friends with the famous Norwegian explorer, Borge Ousland, and asked Borge to help me with training. Borge chose Finse, once used by Scott's great rival Amundsen to train for his successful journey as the first man to reach the South Pole. Finse had a lake to simulate flat-ice travelling when frozen, and conditions not dissimilar to the Antarctic. Misha and I went there in January 2003 on an initial training mission that I concluded was a failure.

We were given a weekend's training with sails, but without two elements of the right equipment, skis and boots. It had been raining the Friday we arrived, and the snow was sticky. None of the training, which combined skiing with sailing, worked for me, and as the weekend progressed, I became more frustrated. On Sunday evening, Misha said he felt he was good enough for Antarctica.

I looked at him and thought, well you might be good enough, but I'm better than you, and I'm not good enough.

It was our first introduction to skiing with sails. At that time, we contemplated doing the Antarctic trip using only sails; the technique for kiting, as I was to discover, was quite different. Having had a weekend of ski sailing in the wrong conditions, and with the wrong equipment, did not convince me I knew enough to start doing it for real in Antarctica, even though Misha thought he was competent. I told him I was going to return and do more training before I could commit to the journey.

What I felt was wrong was that we had been using leather boots and a cross-country binding with skis, and with gusting winds our balance was being changed as the wind blew. We were not gliding along on our skis, and we often stuck. When trying to start to ski while being pulled by a sail, our weight/balance was bound to move forward, and with any sort of wind we fell flat on our faces. After a day of doing that, I was concerned about my inability to use sails. The lines often tangled and I was dragged along the ground. The learning process, such as it was, was frustrating and hard work. This was not helped by the conditions, no good for a beginner, and not having the right skis and boots. It was a cock-up.

The situation had come about because too many people were involved in the decision to go there without first-hand knowledge of what they were advising me about. We used the boots and the skis available at Finse, but they were not the right boots and skis for ski sailing. I did not come home thinking that I had made further progress towards my Antarctic trip.

Fortunately I went to a dinner that Sunday evening in Finse, and one of the men I met there, Thorleif Thorleifsson, was part owner of the local hotel. I told him he was going to see me again because I was not happy at the training I had received. Thorleif said, if you do come back, contact me, and he gave me his card.

I thought about it for a while and did contact him, and told him I had not been happy with the person who had trained me; could he find me someone better to help me? Thorleif said a hotel room was booked for me, gave me a telephone number to contact and told me to talk to the hotel chef, a man called Ronny Finsaas.

Ronny had chosen to live in Finse, the best ski sailing area in Norway, for the past six years purely because he wanted to hone his ski sailing skills. He made his living as a professional chef, but when he was not cooking he was teaching ski sailing and making personal ski sailing expeditions around Finse.

He was among the best in the world at this method of travel.

All this I learned later. I went back to Finse in March 2003, six weeks after my disappointing first training session, and Ronny was the most helpful person possible. He taught me properly on the first day about using sails. I was still struggling, because at that time I was still using cross-country bindings on my skis, where the heel rises on the ski. We thought, mistakenly, that we needed a non-fixed heel binding, to allow us to both ski and walk, but that was ignorance. It was difficult to ski sail with a non-fixed heel.

At this time I was planning the Antarctic journey with just one companion, my Russian friend Misha, though I was also considering a second companion, a friend who lived locally to me in England called Glenn Morris. Glenn, normally a forester, had done several Arctic ski trips, and had skied across Greenland a couple of times. I asked him if he had any appetite for coming to Antarctica? He said he had never considered it, because he would not normally be able to afford it (as it happened, I would have subsidised him, but we never got around to talking money). In the meantime, I told him, I was off to Norway to do some training. Did he want to come over with me to see how we got on? Glenn saw it as a learning situation, whether or not he went on to the Antarctic, and came.

The first day had gone reasonably well, and Ronny suggested making a 40-kilometre journey the following day using skis and sails, down the valley to the village of Outaoset. I thought this was ambitious, and was hesitant. But I was also impressed by the confidence he had that I could do it, so I agreed. We had to get up at 6 o'clock in the morning and start early, in order to finish the trip by 2 o'clock in the afternoon to catch the train back up to our village.

By chance, there was a set of fixed ski-bindings available, and as we prepared for the journey, I asked if I could use them. The difference between using fixed-bindings and cross-country bindings was enormous, and it suddenly all made sense. I found I could do something easily that I had thought, the previous day, was really difficult. Not only did I not need cross-country ski-bindings, I then learned I could use Telemark bindings, which enabled me to have a fixed-heel or not have a fixed heel if I did not need it. Ronny and I did those 40 kilometres in six hours over the mountain ranges of Norway, which was a huge boost to my confidence. This was not a flat area but included mountains, and travelling with skis, being pulled by a sail, was extremely testing. But more than anything, it was fun.

"I'm on for Antarctica," I said later that day.

Glenn, who still used cross-country bindings, did not feel competent enough to continue, and turned his back on Antarctica. He had other ambitions for trips to the Arctic. Even if I had not found another person to join Misha and me to make the Antarctic trip, I had got to the point where I was confident I could do it, because of that vital experience of using sails with skis. I passed the news on to Misha that I was ready to go.

Misha, however, like Robert Swan, was contemplating a different agenda.

In May 2003, he came over to London to see me, and said he wanted to be a politician!

This was a novel reason for refusing to go to Antarctica, and one I am sure few others have heard. Misha said he had stood for the Russian *Duma* – their Parliament – once before, and had failed to get elected. Another election was coming up on December 7, 2003, when we were due to be in Antarctica. Because the person who had won the last election in his region had died, Misha fancied his chances and was going to stand for election again.

"Could you delay the trip?" he asked me.

He knew I had to be in Antarctica by the end of November, and win or lose his election, he promised to get there by mid-December. Would I delay for two or three weeks?

"No," I said, "I won't."

I was funding this expedition, and I dearly wanted it to succeed. That meant I wanted to do it at the best possible time. There were always delays getting into and out of Antarctica, and I needed to be confident that I could get down there early enough, towards the end of November, so if there was a delay I would still be in place by the first or second week of December.

The scope of my ambition had changed since Robert Swan had dropped out. I was less interested in spending forty days on the ice than with doing a specific journey, and I had plumped for a trek from the South Pole to the nearest sea coast, Hercules Inlet. In my mind I allowed 30-odd days to do the actual journey. With any delay, there was a fair chance I would fail to complete before the end of January. I did not want to be hanging around Antarctica, worrying about whether I was going to make the end of January deadline. Conditions started to deteriorate in February.

I had to say no to Misha.

While I was not prepared to change, I had now lost both my potential partners on this expedition, neither through my own fault. Initially, it was the prospect of travelling in their company that had excited me. Robert never really signed on to the trip, other than agreeing to review it again in March 2002. He had bought the concept, but I did not feel let down by Robert. He just was not able to make it. I was more upset at losing Misha, having paid for Misha's training in Kilimanjaro and Norway. For a whole year, when I dreamed about doing the expedition, Misha had been a central part of it. Now he was falling away because he wanted to be a politician!

In reality, of course, it was another trade that had gone wrong. I had to move on. I liked Misha and I still like him. But as one of the most able expedition explorers in the world, I had looked at him as an insurance policy. To have him alongside would have been a comfort, and take some of the risk out of the trip.

I was now just six months away from the most difficult physical expedition of my life, having lost both partners. Whichever way it turned out, I wanted it to succeed, but I could not set off on my own from the South Pole, and walk to the coast. I had no experience of that kind of expedition.

I rang Thorleif Thorleifsson again in Norway, the hotel-owner who employed Ronny Finsaas as a chef. It was only courtesy to speak to Thorleif first.

"How would you feel if I invited Ronny to join me in Antarctica?" I asked him. "Would you be prepared to release him?"

"When are you going?" Thorleif asked.

"We'll be there in November, December, and a little bit of January."

"I'd be proud to let him go," said Thorleif, "but I must tell you that the hotel is closed in November and December, so Ronny is a free agent. I am sure he would be very pleased to be asked."

I asked Thorleif not to tell Ronny I was making these enquiries, because I needed to be absolutely certain Misha was going to take the political option. When Misha confirmed that he was, I rang Ronny.

"Would you like to come to Antarctica? If you can just get yourself down to South America, from then on the trip is funded."

Ronny could not believe it, and said he thought that Christmas had come early. This brought me back to two of us on the trip, and I began to feel it was actually coming together better than the original plan. I rationalised Misha's absence by telling myself that his skills had been honed in the Arctic, not the Antarctic. He had never done a trip in the Antarctic, and did not have any genuine kite or sail experience. With Ronny I had someone with the greatest experience of kite and sail. At 30, he was young and fit. I concluded that having Ronny join me had not retarded the journey. He had genuinely helped me so much that I was really pleased I could give him the opportunity.

All the actual organising for the trip was still being done by Anne Kershaw's ANI, a company that specialised in such journeys. She and I had a discussion about who might be available to assist on the navigation in Antarctica, to become a third member of my party. There seemed to be two choices. One was Paul Landry, based up in northern Canada, who had done kiting and sailing in Greenland and Baffin Island. The other was Geoff Somers, who had actually been on a trip with Robert Swan in 1996, and had done a four thousand mile trans-Antarctic journey in 1989/90. He was very experienced in Antarctica, and had won an MBE for his Polar skills.

I thought it was necessary to have someone with intimate experience of Antarctica, rather than another person with ski sailing experience only. Ronny, however skilful he was, had never been out of Norway; he could ski sail but he did not know the southern terrain. Anne pressed the case for Paul Landry, who had done a lot of ski sailing and was keen to come. My problem with Paul was that I was not going to meet him very frequently in the preparation. On the other hand, I had met Geoff Somers in 1995 on my "tourist" trip to the South Pole, and he did live in England, even though it was in Keswick, the other end of the country from me. I contacted Geoff, and asked him to consider the trip. He did not agree immediately, because he wanted to see how it would fit in with other things he had planned. At that time he was assisting Rosie Stancer, the distant cousin of the Queen, preparing her to walk from Patriot Hills to the South Pole. Geoff knew he would have to go down south anyway at the end of the year to finish her preparation and see her off. After some discussion we came to a financial arrangement, and it was eventually decided that he was on the team.

Geoff Somers brought immense experience to the expedition, as one of the world's most accomplished Polar travellers. He had completed several "firsts" including the then-longest unsupported Arctic journey, 1,400 miles traversing by dog sled from the South to the North of the Greenland Ice Cap. He had trained the successful all-women team to both the North and South Poles, but he was not exclusively a cold-weather traveller. He had crossed Borneo, for example, through untravelled jungle, and in Australia, along with three wild camels, travelled by foot the 1,400 miles between Perth and Ayers Rock, known as the "Red Centre" of the continent. I was fortunate to get him.

Originally, I was paying Anne, through ANI, a block of money to make everything happen. The funding paid for a number of resources, including sledges. I planned to spend the summer of 2003 on holiday in southern Spain with my family, but just before I left Anne sent me an e-mail saying she had resigned as the chairman of ANI, which was one of seven travel companies brought together under one group, based in America. She did not give a detailed explanation for her departure, but ANI had been an independent company until she had sold it to the Americans, after which she fell out with them and left. The Americans assured me then that this would not make any difference to me, and that everything was still on schedule.

I went away on holiday, with my family to Spain. At this time my fitness was improving, things were looking great and I was feeling good. When I come back on July 24, I picked up e-mail from Geoff Somers:

*Martin,*

*Hold on to your seat – some disturbing news I am afraid – returned home from a few days away – I have just received a one-liner e-mail from Anne Kershaw stating that ANI will not operate this year in Antarctica!!!! This is a blow to all concerned. Lost you and the others their trip. What a bummer. Shall speak to you....Geoff.*

I do not think I have ever been so devastated.

Everything else I could overcome, people dropping out, equipment failures, holes in a training programme, that sort of thing I had already overcome. But how could I overcome not being able to get to Antarctica? If I could not get in, there was no journey to make. ANI was the only means of doing this, there were no alternatives. The only company that took travellers into that icy continent had arbitrarily decided that, this year, it was not going to do it!

The reason ANI gave was that their bookings were down. A big part of their business was flying groups of people to Antarctica to climb the Vinson Massif – Mount Vinson – 16,960 feet high. Typically, 80 climbers a year would want to summit Mt Vinson. But because 2003 was the 50th anniversary of the first ascent of Everest and there was an excess of climbers repeating that feat, it was thought to be one reason why the climbing fraternity had not booked to climb in Antarctica the same year. ANI had been relying on a regular intake of climbers over the years, and when its new owners suddenly found a big drop in numbers, they decided to shut down for the whole year.

It was possible the new owners of ANI were not really aware of how risky the business was. Accustomed to more traditional travel companies, the Americans may not have realised that there was not even a hotel in Antarctica. The new company felt that with just four months to go to the travelling season, there should have been more deposits paid, and more certainty about their clientele. Cancelling all flights for that season meant no business at all in the base camp in Patriot Hills, the maintenance of which could easily cost two million dollars a season. The company seemed to have felt that if they cancelled the 2003/4 season, all the clients that year would just reschedule for the following year.

*Digging out skis from wind-blown snow before we can travel.*

*Geoff with 10 sqm sail approaching a difficult area.* © *Ronny Finsaas*

*Good conditions allow use of a 14 sqm sail.* © Ronny Finsaas

*Overnight drift.* © *Ronny Finsaas*

*Our first sledge beginning to break up being repaired by Geoff.*

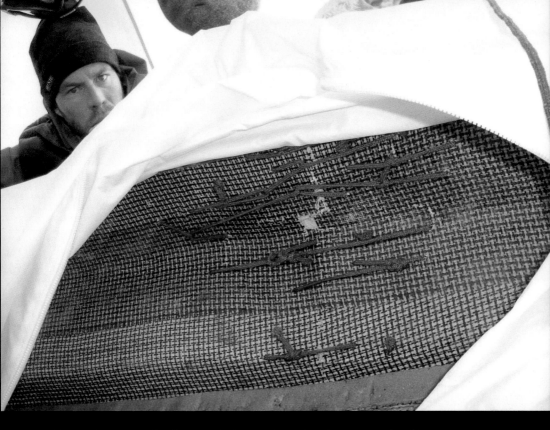

*Concerned Ronny looks over Geoff's first sledge repairs, a job that became familiar.*

*Sastrugi to navigate over.*

*Ronny repairing his sledge. The runner needed several additional bolts, and I wait for the drill to repair my sledge.*

That was no use to me. I was psyched up for 2003. I absolutely did not want to reschedule. Nor did others like the Murray family, the financier Simon Murray who at 63 aimed to be the oldest man to walk to the South Pole with Pen Hadow as his guide, or his wife Jennifer Murray who, with co-pilot Colin Bodill, were attempting to fly around the world in a helicopter via the North and South Poles.

Mike Sharp, my companion in the ski trip across Greenland in 1999, contacted me. When I had met him in 1995, ANI had employed him. He told me he was going to pick up the business cancelled by ANI.

"I'm going to fill their place," he said, "I want to put the business back together."

I was doubtful.

"With respect Mike, I wish you well but I don't think you will," I told him. "Certainly, I am not going to be your first customer."

I had some idea of the enormous task Mike was setting out on, a formidable prospect even though he understood how the base camp at Patriot Hills actually worked. One of Mike's partners already had a project for salvaging an aircraft – a Dakota DC 3 – that had crashed down there; he had bought the aircraft from the insurance company as a basis for a new company. Mike knew his partner was desperate to justify putting a base camp in place. Granted Mike understood the business, and he knew the climber numbers would increase. He would see commitments from the Murrays, and he wanted some commitment from me as part of the package to put the whole deal together. But it was still a proposition that could easily fail. If all the people who said they wanted to go to Antarctica at the end of 2003 expressed a firm interest, Mike thought he would pull it off. I had my doubts. I was nervous about committing myself mentally to it, because I could not live with the thought of putting everything into going and then finding it was physically impossible.

Obviously, though, I was never going to allow Mike to go ahead and not take me with him.

The alternative, of course, was not going.

I had not thought about this seriously, except if I was barred from going. It really was difficult to handle. I did not want to allow myself to be let down twice. Being let down once was bad enough, and I could not be let down again. For weeks, I would not allow myself to hope that Mike was going to succeed, but I stayed in regular weekly contact with him until it looked like he had made sufficient progress.

Seven weeks went by. Mike was still in there, still saying he could make it work, and so one day I took a deep breath and phoned him.

"Mike, it looks like you're going to achieve it. I'm on."

I was encouraging Mike, telling him that if he succeeded, I was on, but during that seven weeks I could not tell him I was on because I did not think he was going to succeed. I did not want to raise my hopes, or his. Obviously I was hopeful. He was open about the risk, whether or not he was going to succeed.

He said, "I think I've done it, but I cannot guarantee I can do it."

When I said to him, I'll send you the deposit, I remember thinking, he's an honourable person, and if he doesn't go ahead, he'll return the money.

I told him that my trip was not being funded by a sponsor, or a charity, or anything like that. It was my own personal money. After travelling with him across Greenland, I considered myself a friend of his. When he said he would not let me down, I did not think he would. He would not have accepted my money if he had not believed he was going to succeed.

He had a terrible struggle that summer organising the new business, but he did very well. I know he needed my support, and from the seventh week he got it. He had been pretty confident that he had verbal commitments. He never got any front money from anyone, but he put the deal together. I was not the first to commit, because I would not allow myself to commit.

This led to problems with my own expedition.

In my schedule Geoff Somers was going off in early November, that is, only five or six weeks after I committed to Mike Sharp. The difference between what Mike was offering and what Anne had offered was that Anne had promised infrastructure, sledges and other equipment already down in Antarctica, having been supplied for a previous expedition, and I was going to use those. But all Mike Sharp wanted to be involved in was getting us into Antarctica, and out afterwards. No sledges were included in the deal.

I had to go back to Geoff to say I needed further help.

"Can you do the extra preparation?" I asked him. "Can you get sledges, new sledges?"

He said it would mean another five or six weeks paid work, which I agreed, and that it was going to take six weeks to get new sledges made and delivered. I said we should be able to make that deadline, and immediately sent him the extra money for the new sledges.

When I sent Geoff that money, I was committed, even though at the back of my mind I knew that new sledges could always be saved for another year if that was how things went and Mike did fail.

I was now having a problem with insurance, because of that ill-fated trip two years earlier when two ski sailors had to be rescued, and insurance companies paid out hundreds of thousands of dollars. As a natural result, insurers did not like ski sailing.

The British Mountaineering Club had insured me on other journeys. This time they said, sorry, we do not do that any more. I asked why and they said, not in so many words, that they considered anything involving sails and kites was a stunt. If you are walking, they said, you are walking, if you are man-hauling a sledge, you are man-hauling, and both these situations we know how to judge the risk and can insure against them. But if you are relying on sails, there are two types of risk we have not been able to assess. One is the risk of personal injury, the other is the risk of being weather-bound. They linked us with that unsuccessful attempt two years earlier.

I had to have some form of insurance, otherwise I would not even be allowed into Antarctica. I asked Mike Sharp what I should do. Could he recommend anyone?

Mike recommended a company who, when I read their insurance cover, had allocated just five thousand pounds for rescue.

"This isn't any good," I told Mike. "That money wouldn't even begin to cover a rescue."

He said other people used it. I contacted the insurance company broker, and told them I was never going to be lost, because I had a GPS, which would always tell me where I was. It would not be "search and rescue", I told them, just rescue.

"What would happen if you don't get rescued?" he asked.

"Well, I would run out of food and ultimately die."

"Exactly," he said, "and that is when the medical bit clicks in, because there's two and a half million dollars of medical insurance."

I do not believe that, I thought, but if that was what they were saying, they can go with it. I asked Mike if he was happy with that kind of insurance.

"I am asking," I told him, "because if I need to be rescued, I am not going to be paying three hundred thousand dollars. The insurance company will pay it, or you won't get it. Are you prepared to accept that policy?"

He said he was. I asked him to put it in writing that he was prepared to accept that policy. He did so. That was another risk he took. He and his three partners did that deal by the seat of their pants. Mike is a real character, and we need more risk-takers like that.

Meanwhile, Ronny was taking very seriously his job of finding the right size sails to travel with. It came down to three sizes, depending on the wind strength, the smallest of 5 square metres, an intermediate of 10 square metres, and a big one for light winds of 14 square metres.

Then Ronny dropped his own bombshell.

"I think we should take a kite!" he said.

"I have never flown a kite before," I said, doubtfully. "Aren't they much different from sails? Doesn't the sail have just 20 foot lines, while a kite's lines go out to 150 feet?"

Ronny agreed they were different, but he had skied with them both and he thought kites were necessary. Kites were used in very light winds because they worked at a much greater height than sails, and there was almost always more wind above 100 feet than at ice surface level. I tried to establish if there was a reasonable minimum wind in which a sail could be used, because I did not want to have to go on to the ice at the South Pole and use a kite for real with no practice at all. If we stuck with sails, I thought we could get by. Ronny did not. He said we needed a greater ability to move in lighter winds, and we had no alternative to a kite.

I was hesitant, but Ronny was the expert. If he said we needed a kite we each had to take one. He said he would send one over from Norway so I could take it out into the fields and play with it. It arrived and I went out one day when there was little wind, but enough to get the kite up in the air. It proved difficult to control, and I could not see myself doing it with a set of skis, let alone towing a sledge and travelling 700 miles with it. It was a nice sunny day when I practiced, and the idea of sorting out 50 metre lines, and doing it in temperatures of minus 40 with all my gear on, and making it work for me, well, I thought, this could be tricky. After two hour's practice the kite crashed into a tree; the lines are still there today. I had to tell Ronny that he would get his kite back, but without any lines. My confidence dropped. I did not feel adequately prepared. I half-hoped I would only have to use the kite at the beginning.

In late October, Mike Sharp dropped me another blow. He was not certain when he could actually get me to the South Pole.

"I can get you into Antarctica at the end of November, that is, to base camp at Patriot Hills," he told me, "but I do not have enough fuel to get you to the South Pole. I will need the fuel I already have, to ensure I can always rescue the people that I have already put in there, those who are doing the walking."

He told me that he might not be able to get me in until December 10, and actually would prefer to put me in on December 29. I said that was unacceptable.

"I don't want to go then. I want to get in early."

"Well, I haven't got enough fuel," he replied.

"There's fuel down there," I pointed out.

"Yes, but it's not mine. It's ANI's."

I rang ANI. They were aware at this stage what Mike was doing. I asked them how they felt about him picking up business that they had abandoned.

"Obviously a few of your clients whom you were hoping to go next year with you, are going instead this year with Mike," I said. "Are you upset?"

They said they were not really upset, but were interested in how Mike did, and whether or not he would succeed.

"So you don't really resent it?" I asked.

They said, no.

"In that case," I said, "would you mind selling him some fuel to help him?"

They said they would consider doing that.

I went back to Mike and said that I understood why he was not talking to them, because he felt he was treading on their toes. But I had found that they did not resent what he was doing, and he could negotiate with them for fuel. Some of that fuel, I told him, could be used to get me to the Pole when I wanted to go, and not when it was convenient for Mike.

A week went by. Mike came on the line.

"I can get you to the Pole, when do you want to go?"

"Thanks," I said.

In the deal, Mike came to a financial arrangement with ANI, and took on their whole business in the Antarctic. He was obviously prepared to take the risk. They were not.

In all the journeys I had done so far, I had maximum support from my wife, Christina. She did not encourage me to do them, but believed that as the worst happened to only good people, I would always come back! Her view was, I was a survivor. She came to the view that she need not worry too much about me going off and leaving her with our two daughters. I always felt she was in control but ahead of this journey across Antarctica, I did sense more anxiety than on previous trips.

My eldest daughter, Isabel, then 18, felt responsibility for the family and was uneasy with the thought that I was being "selfish".

This upset me. I asked my youngest daughter, Marina, if she felt the same way. She replied, "Daddy, if you want to do it, do it, but make sure you come home."

I explained to Isabel that she would do a lot of things in her life that I would not necessarily approve of, and asked her to allow me to do this.

She eventually agreed. It was a difficult day.

My wife Christina was detached about me going and accepted it.

Then Geoff told me we had three sledges, but they were not new. Each sledge had only done one trip before and they were, he said, *as good* as new; the sledges' previous use had only been a light trip in the Arctic. Geoff assured me they were fine. I thought if he was happy, and said they were good enough, they were good enough.

Now we had all the equipment. Geoff went down south early. Not only was he preparing the food supplies, much of which he bought in Punta Arenas, he was also dealing with last-minute matters for Rosie Stancer as well as me. I asked Ronny to go down to Punta Arenas a few days earlier than me, so he could join Geoff, whom he had only met once before, and get to know him. I wanted him to ensure that all the equipment that he was bringing down was OK. Geoff took his equipment with him, and Ronny, who came to London and stayed with me, took his equipment too. I drove Ronny to the airport on November 20. Four days later I followed on down. I had just my own personal ski gear, skis, and clothes. Ronny had taken the sails and kites down. Geoff had taken the sledges and the food. I came down with the satellite telephones and the solar panel.

It did not help that some of my teeth started to fall out, and my back had become a serious worry.

# 7

# At the South Pole

I travelled from Heathrow to San Paulo in Brazil, carrying excess baggage and getting an upgrade to First Class. The flight took off two hours late at 11.30am on November 26, 2003. I was full of enthusiasm, optimistic, with a strong sense of "at last it's happening". Yet even though I was flying south, it was still not certain that I could fly in and out of Antarctica to get the trip done. Any delays in the Antarctic were long ones.

I was also apprehensive that, having got through all my problems and put everything into place, I had to follow through. Would I be allowed to do that? I had to hope for a fair wind.

The first setback hit me the following day, flying from San Paulo to Santiago in Chile, when two of my teeth implants fell out.

Teeth were often casualties on Polar journeys. I had broken teeth in the past, which was uncomfortable and painful. My teeth were at risk primarily from eating frozen food, or trying to eat chocolate. Cheese could be rock hard in sub-zero temperatures. Altitude affected teeth, in that small bubbles between fillings could expand and blow out the fillings. Knowing the altitude at the Pole, I had taken every precaution to make sure that my teeth were in the best condition possible. Over an eighteen-month period in England, I had extensive dentistry work done. I had spent thousands on implants; why should I have teeth problems when so much else was at risk? The dentist took out all the weaknesses in my mouth, such as bridges, the leaning of one tooth on another.

You can imagine how I felt on the aircraft, looking at two pieces of porcelain – my new teeth implants lying in my hand. I was furious that this should happen when I was entering a foreign country, and not where I could call my own dentist and have them repaired.

In Santiago I had four hours in hand before catching an aircraft south to Punta Arenas. What could I do about my teeth? The first plane to fly into Antarctica had been due to leave Punta Arenas on November 25, with a second aircraft due out five days later. I had a place booked on the second aircraft, but it was now November 27 and I knew the first aircraft had not yet left. If I could get down there on time, catching the link aircraft within four hours, I might manage to get on the first plane. But with two teeth in my hand I felt certain I would not get down to Punta Arenas until gone midnight. Even if I worked quickly and organised a dentist there for the following day, (the day the first aircraft was leaving), I would miss it.

What could I do in Santiago in four hours?

At the information desk the young woman there spoke very little English and was no help. But a man standing next to me, an American, waiting for his parents told me he had seen a dentist in the airport.

"I'll take you to it!" he said.

Within ten minutes I was sitting in a dentist's chair and within half an hour I had had my implants back in, glued solidly. Though the implants had fallen out, the steel core of the teeth had remained in the gum. They were still solid, rooted into my bone, and he fixed the porcelain teeth so they have not moved since (much later my London dentist said how well they had been done). To cheer me up, it cost a fraction of the price it would have cost in London. I was able to catch the next aircraft to Punta Arenas, meeting up with Geoff Somers and Ronny Finsass, and all our gear.

Next day, November 28, we were up at 0630 ready for a call to fly to the Antarctic base camp at Patriot Hills. We were set to leave at 0700, but it was too windy to take off. There were updates on 0900, 1100, 1400, 1900 and 2100 and at the end of that day, no go. I had lunch with Geoff and Ronny, feeling in a state of repressed excitement, and did some shopping. There was a bronze statue of the great Portuguese seaman and navigator, Magellan, and Antarctic travellers kissed the statue for good luck, which we did. We had heard that the Russian aircrew we were using had never flown into Antarctica, and there was some nervousness that Ilyushin aircraft were not able to operate in the high cross-winds tolerated by the sturdy American Hercules aircraft. That evening I drank cokes with Geoff, and listened to a few of his Antarctic stories. We had an early night, but I had to acknowledge the fact my back pain was getting worse and I was suffering.

I had not owned up to this to Geoff or Ronny, and I planned to suffer my way through it. Six months into the two and a half years training for the Antarctic journey I had incurred an injury that, on and off, had been a problem on a skiing holiday in Zermatt, it was so bad I could not ski, and I had to spend a couple of days walking around town. The part of my back that hurt was right at the bottom, near the coccyx. I could sit down but sometimes I could not bend my back at all. Physiotherapists and chiropractors had done little good. I continued training, expecting to live with the pain. Sometimes training helped it, even running. Two or three weeks before I left for the Antarctic, my back deteriorated further. Buried deep in my mind I was fearful; how was I ever going to pull a sledge in such a condition?

There was really no one to talk to about it. What would be the point in telling someone when I was going ahead anyway? Either people would think I was making an excuse in case anything went wrong; or they may have seen it as an opening move to call the trip off. Obviously, thirty-two hours on the plane going down to South America had not improved things.

On arrival at Punta Arenas I heard of a masseur. He worked out of a hair-dresser's, which did not sound promising, and it sounded even more dubious that he was a blind Chilean. I went there anyway on November 29, on the principle that beggars cannot be choosers. I had to physically point out on his back what was wrong with my back. He spent ten minutes working on my back, guided solely by what I had pointed out on his back, and then spent fifty minutes on my feet. In all, it was an hour's treatment, for the princely sum of $8.00.

I immediately felt an improvement.

It took me some time to assess how big an improvement he had made. That one's hour's treatment was effective for five months, and carried me through the whole Antarctic journey. It was astonishing.

Getting my teeth repaired and visiting the blind masseur with such pleasing results, made me start to believe there was an element of destiny in setting out on the journey from the South Pole. It was as if someone, outside of my consciousness, was looking after me and wanted to smooth my path.

I spent the evening putting co-ordinates into my GPS, dreaming of the journey ahead.

At 10.30 on the evening of November 30 we flew out of Punta Arenas, arriving at Patriot Hills, our Antarctic base camp, at 3 o'clock in the morning, Chilean time. By 5.30 we had unloaded and put up our tent. We went to sleep at 0800, but I slept just three hours.

Time in the Antarctic was a relative thing, and there were four different times. The US base station, Scott/Amundsen, got its supplies from McMurdo Station, which was supplied from New Zealand, so they used NZ time. We had already been using Chilean time, 5-½ hours behind GMT, and base camp – Patriot Hills – was also using Chilean time, therefore we had to be aware of the time in Chile. There was always GMT, Greenwich Mean Time, when we referred to home. But actually we were going to ski on local time, and local time was when, at midnight, the sun was directly behind us. At that time of year there were 24 hours of daylight and no natural night. Because we had a kite or a sail in the air, we wanted the sun behind us all the time we were skiing. Looking up at the sail meant looking at the sky as well, and into Antarctic sunshine this would be wearing, even dangerous. To get a maximum day, perhaps ten hours travelling, we needed to ski through the "night", that is from 7 o'clock in the evening until 5 o'clock the following morning. Midnight would be the middle of our day. In the Southern Hemisphere, the sun obviously still rose in the east and set in the west, but at mid-day was directly to the north. We were going to be heading north to get to Hercules Inlet.

We woke at Patriot Hills at 1100 hrs Chilean time, and I went ski sailing with Ronny while Geoff saw off Rosie Stancer. The sailing was good fun but the wind was gusting strongly, and we were down to our smallest 5 SqM sail to cope. Later we prepared our sledges. Dinner was at 1900 and it was an early night for me at 2300. I rang home to say I had arrived safely.

For the next twenty-four hours through December 1 we were subjected to winds of 70 mph. I spent time building walls around the tent I shared with Ronny; his half of the wall looked better than mine but it was blown over while we had lunch in Geoff's tent. We had considered taking two tents with us on the journey with one as a back up, but that night, with both tents rigged, the guidelines were torn away from the canvas of my tent, and some of the poles in Geoff's tent buckled. We thought we could live with the buckled poles, but the torn guidelines obviously made my tent not worth taking. Geoff said we should take only one tent, a decision that turned out to be fortuitous. We did not realise it at the time, but the poles of the second tent would not have fitted easily on to the sledges, and would have been awkward when they overturned. Conditions we subsequently met with our sledges, and the damage the sledges endured, could all have been much worse.

That meant three of us were going to use a single three-man tent – something of a tight squeeze. One compensation was that it was much warmer, because Geoff's tent, coloured yellow, allowed the sunrays to come through.

I practiced sailing with the 10 SqM sail. Later I rang my mother, and Isabel at university. We completed the preparation of our sledges and bubble-wrapped forty litres of fuel to protect it from knocks and spillage. What we needed was a window of good weather to make that final flight to the Pole.

I went to sleep suffering from a headache induced by the noise of the wind hitting the tent. It turned out to be a good night, and the wind began to slacken.

On December 2, we made the startling discovery that the tent Ronny and I were using was 15 degrees colder than Geoff's, which reconfirmed it would be his tent that would protect all three of us. We glued together his tent poles to make it quicker to rig the tent, I did some ski sailing at lunchtime, and Geoff, more at home on kites, did some of his first work that afternoon with sails. I found that two pairs of socks were better than three, but was still searching for the right combination of gloves, as my fingers became cold.

Mike Sharp asked me to supply him with an emergency contact number should it be necessary. I gave him my wife, Christina, although I would not wish a call like that on anyone.

We watched Simon Murray set off with Pen Hadow to walk to the Pole. Simon, 63, was aiming to be the oldest man ever to make this journey. He was in a competition of adventures with his wife, Jennifer, who was also going to the South Pole with her flying companion Colin Bodill, but in a helicopter, as one leg of a flight around the world via the North and South Poles.

Ronny was easy to share a tent with. I wondered how we would cope, three to a tent, and something of a squeeze. My nose kept running. I did not have a cold but I could not stop it happening; it was irritating, nothing more. I was going to shave every day, so there was not going to be a moustache for my nose to run into. Geoff was sceptical that the electric razor I was taking would last out the journey without its batteries going flat. I was more confident.

Geoff, who cooked dinner, told me we needed to spend one or two days at the Pole to acclimatise to the altitude. We got into our sleeping bags at 2100, determined to rise at 0600 the following day, scheduled to start our flight from Patriot Hills to the Pole at 1000 hrs. I heard that the Americans at the Scott/Amundsen Base at the Pole had invited us to look at their Antarctic Station. They had for years been hostile to all travellers, but this attitude had changed in recent years.

At 1005 on December 3, 2003 we left Patriot Hills just five minutes behind schedule. We landed at Thiel Mountains, a fuel cache, to re-fuel at 1233, left just over an hour later at 1341, and at last, the end of one stage and the beginning of the real journey after two and a half years preparation, we arrived at the South Pole at 1556; the outside temperature was minus 38c degrees.

It took us four hours to make camp and have dinner and later went off to the American scientific station and spoke to weathermen, the head of operations, passport and souvenir offices. They went out of their way to be hospitable and encouraged us to see their work. We were the first expeditioners they had seen that year, because we were travelling from the Pole. Others walking to the Pole would get there some months later.

I started to feel really ill.

I was facing a ski journey of 607 miles over ice and mountain in temperatures often below minus 30, and I felt dreadful. After all I had done to prepare for this journey I couldn't believe it. Ronny had never been at altitude. He felt fine. Geoff had already explained that he often felt muzzy on arrival at the South Pole, but that did not incapacitate him. On previous trip to the Pole I had felt fine, and I had done my Kilimanjaro training. Of the three of us, surely I would cope with altitude?

But I was not coping. I felt incapacitated.

Back at our tent at 1.30am, I felt worse still. This was a real downer. As I did whenever I was ill, I started to ask, when was I going to get better? How on earth was I going to ski 607 miles when I could hardly lift my head off the pillow?

Geoff suggested a very English solution.

"Go for a walk," he said.

I took his advice; anything to feel better. Obviously, with the temperature outside, even at the base station, people did not often take a walk. But as I tried to walk off my illness I saw a distant figure, so naturally gravitated in that direction. It was a woman. She had heard that we had arrived at the base, and as she was a keen backcountry skier in the United States, she wanted to see the equipment we were using. Her name was Molly Hutspilher, an American in her forties. I explained that I was suffering from altitude sickness, and like a miracle, she turned out to be the base station doctor. Molly told me to follow her back to the base medicentre. There she gave me two full litres of saline, injected directly into my veins, along with four hours of oxygen, a bowl of soup and two steroid tablets for swelling.

I soon became a different man.

All the sickness went away. It was astonishing that I should meet Molly. She told me it could have taken a week to recover from altitude sickness. Normally, the cure would be to reduce in height, but at the South Pole I could not do that; it was a high plateau above 9,000 feet, there was no dropping down.

Why was I lucky enough to find the station doctor when I was in so much need of a cure? On my own, without that encounter, I would not have dreamt of going to the Americans to ask for help. We were an independent expedition on a private trip, and it was not a requirement of the Americans to help us. I did not want to ask them for the use of any facilities. Not that they would not give, but I did not want to ask. Other people felt the same way. We were doing our own trip, and would be parted from the Americans soon. We would not have their assistance then and I felt we should not ask for it at the Pole. They just happened to be there.

When I got back to Geoff and Ronny and said I was ready to set off on our trek, but I still had apprehensions, but we lined up to take our individual photographs next to the exact South Pole, surrounded by the flags of a number of nations. I was glad to get going.

A major factor in leaving quickly was the weather, a lovely 14-knot wind that could carry us a decent distance on our first day's travelling. At that strength I would be able to use a sail, with which I was familiar. I would not have to use a kite, which I was worried about using. I wanted to get away while the wind was strong enough for sails.

That day we did 16.2 nautical miles. The wind averaged 12 knots, perfect for ski sailing, but the sastrugi, the surface over which we were skiing, was the worst that Geoff had ever seen on the plateau in five similar journeys. I had heard that on the Plateau itself there was little wind, leaving the snow surface relatively smooth. This was the good news, the bad news was that there had been excessive wind in the winter season, and the sastrugi was blown into frozen wavelengths, with one to three feet between peak and trough. It was difficult to ski over and took its toll on equipment and our bodies. Full of adrenaline, I was happy to ski for just five hours, not a full day, and cover sixteen nautical miles. I was relieved and happy and had recovered from being ill. Optimism was high, we were on our way, and I did not feel tired. We were all glad to have got away from the Pole.

It was that evening that I learned a lesson in tent manners when I asked for the three extra inches of space I had been allowed on the first night at the Pole, which invited Geoff's derision at the cooking stove.

The cooking was always the same. We ate boil-in-a-bag stuff, pasta and some form of meat. It was freeze-dried food, with powdered potato. If we could mix it with water, we had it.

Each meal started with a hot drink, made immediately we set up the tent, having already that day drunk any hot liquids stored in our thermos. Geoff put water on to boil as soon as possible. We had powdered soup which I particularly liked, and if I could get a second helping, I would.

Cooking was done on a spirit stove, not pressure-cooking. We had two stoves, one as a spare, so simple they were incapable of breaking down, and there was little weight to them. We had two cooking pots. Geoff would make everything from a big cooking pot with boiled water, pouring the freeze-dried food into it. He took his meal in a mug, I had mine out of a bowl and Ronny would have the balance out of the pot.

Every other day we ate salami as a starter. It was our individual choice. We had an allocation of food – cheese, salami, nuts and chocolate, lots of chocolate – and it was up to each of us when we wanted to eat it. Geoff did not like eating during the day. I might eat salami with breakfast. Ronny would save his salami until the end of the day. We could, in our rules, break into next day's rations for these luxuries, but obviously we would be short the following day. We had plenty of food, chosen for calorific value, 4,800 calories a day.

Afterwards we drank coffee with dried milk if we wanted milk with it. We also enjoyed a Chilean hot fruit drink that was very popular which we drank in the morning. Geoff and Ronny carried this fruit drink in their thermos flasks each day, while I preferred to carry water.

After we had eaten, we talked over the day's progress and wondered what the following day would be like. We talked about anything; schooldays was one subject, wrote our diaries, compared notes with our GPS's, and we read. I had a Joe Simpson book with me, and Roy Jenkins' biography of Winston Churchill. Most days as soon as we had eaten, I wanted to go to sleep. Geoff would walk around the outside of the tent in his bare feet. I did it once. I tried this a couple of times.

When I went to bed I always left my inner layer of clothing on. It was not cold enough to justify more than one inner layer, long johns and vest. There

Radiation in the tent created a temperature of  15C (60F), outside the temperature is minus 30C (-22F).

*Ronny with sawn-off sastrugi, our water for the evening.*

*Not all repairs could be done inside our tent. Geoff wishing he could work with his gloves on.*

*Kites ready, Monday, Dec 22, as we exchange old sledges for new.*

*Ready to go with new exchange sledge.*

A time of great anxiety for me, the Pilot Karl had delivered our replacement sledges and was now checking his take off area to avoid any large sastrugi. I felt responsible if anything were to go wrong

*A regular event. First, our sledges roll over, then our 50 metres kite lines catch on sastrugi. We detach ourselves completely from our sledges and walk to untangle lines.*

*Passing Thiel Mountains in 10 miles of new soft snow.*

were times when I took them off. I emphatically did not want to sweat and make my sleeping bag wet.

Ironically, the sleeping bag did not go outside while the cooking was going on, despite the advice of Misha in Russia. The difference between the Arctic and Antarctica was that it was warm in the tent in Antarctica, because we had sunrays 24 hours a day. Typically, it was 60 degrees Fahrenheit without cooking heat in our yellow tent. With the stove on, the temperature rose to 70 degrees. No damp got to our sleeping bags.

We did not do any washing of clothes, but we probably could have done. Drying was not a problem; it freeze-dried. The most fantastic thing about Antarctica was that I could put a flannel out to dry, which during the night would become solid. By the morning I could just roll it up in my hands, and it would become crisp and refreshing.

A Thermos ridge rest was part of our bedding, our mattress. The first layer protecting us from the ice surface was the ground sheet, integral to the tent. On top of that, we put down a thin layer of foam going across the whole of the tent, which kept some heat in it, then we laid an individual ridge-rest, and on top of that we each had a blow-up mattress, about an inch thick. In Antarctica, the dry humidity there allowed a blow-up mattress to work much better than it did in the Arctic, where the air freezes. With these layers underneath us, we then put down our sleeping bags.

A normal ridge rest was 18 inches wide, but Ronny's was 24 inches wide. I had seen this extra-wide ridge-rest in the shop in England, but thought it was too selfish of me to have one and thought it would not easily go into the bags and on to the sledge anyway.

Ronny is such a good chap I thought, that I genuinely didn't mind him having that bit of extra space.

But it was ironic that Ronny's ridge rest turned into a superb armchair, of which I was very jealous. I had taken a smaller and restrictive chair to sit on, but sitting in the tent was not comfortable.

Geoff always wanted eight hours sleep. He wanted to wake at 4pm, so he could be in bed at 8am. We would finish travelling at 5am and made camp by 6am. The cooking was done by 7.

I went to sleep much later. I probably only needed 6 hours sleep. Ronny slept as much as he could.

In our mornings Geoff woke first, then it would be me. I did not need an alarm clock.

Going to the toilet, especially the all-important – and hopefully only – constitutional, we wanted to do in our mornings. We used pee bottles to avoid the need to get out of a warm sleeping bag in the middle of our "night" and go out into the cold, to pee. Ronny did not mind doing that. Conditions certainly made me want to pee all the time. We wanted to do as little environmental damage as possible. Each day we picked up any litter, not that there was much of it, to ensure we left the site as pristine as possible, even if it was seen by no one else in a thousand years.

# 8

# Saturday, December 6, 2003

My breakfast on December 6 was the previous night's dinner I had not eaten because I fell asleep, cold pasta and freeze-dried meat. It had the calories I needed. I kept my normal breakfast – salami, chocolate and cheese – as provisions on my sledge.

Looking out of the tent, there was little wind, much like the previous day. We got away from camp at 1830, and for the first 2-½ hours travelled only a hundred yards. It seemed like we were constantly lifting the kites or bringing them down to wait for the wind to emerge. There came a point where we became very cold, and faced an important decision; do we hang on and get even colder hoping the wind will come, or do we pitch tent and get warm inside it? We decided to pitch tent.

None of us could travel; it had nothing to do with my kiting skills, poor at the time.

We had lunch, always the same, chocolate, nuts, cheese and salami. Then a wind sprang up. We broke camp immediately and set off again, and during the rest of the day covered 24 miles. We were chuffed. The temperature increased and that made a difference, because we were struggling with our hands and feet, both parts where there were problems with the cold. We each had similar boots and had been told the linings would be sufficient to keep out the cold, but they were not. When the temperature dropped below minus 30, our feet got cold. Once the temperature rose above minus 27, our feet improved. None of us, though, suffered from frostbite, no black toes. But we knew we could not hang around too long, and had to keep working. I kept adjusting my boots and gloves. I started by wearing three pairs of socks, and got down to wearing only one pair, and loosening the boots a bit. This gave a lot more circulation to my feet when I was working, as it meant they could generate warmth themselves.

We used sails to cover the whole of the 24 miles travelled that day, with winds up to 16 knots, perfect for ski sailing. But we had to make changes to our harnesses by tying ropes to all the straps. One problem working with sails and kites was that our harness became loose, and we could not pull it tight enough with gloves, because it would not stay in position. To counter this, we made holes in all our straps and tied ropes to them; it gave us a lot more leverage on the strap. Each time we stopped we could give the ropes a tug and retighten our harness. Having a tough surface to ski over compounded the problem.

It was a good day. I had expected to do 80 miles in the first five days, and mentally I had prepared myself for that. To have done 45 miles in three days was good, on schedule, so I was happy, the more so in that having a decent wind on the second part of that day meant I did not have to use the kite.

That evening, just twenty-four hours after Geoff's derision about my request for an extra three inches of space, an attempt was made to allocate me more room. Depending on how we messed down in the tent, sometimes the extra room seemed to be there, sometimes it was not. The difference was, could I put a cup down? Was there anywhere to put my hot drink? Most of the time, space was available so I was able to get a hot drink down.

It is not difficult to imagine my feelings when, at the other end of the tent that night where Geoff was cooking, the stove burned a hole in his rubber mattress, which went flat. It transpired that the metal protector that went around the stove had not been fitted properly. We had a long journey to complete, and on this, only our third day, Geoff had a flat mattress! I felt guilty. It was not my fault that the metal protector had not been fitted properly, but had there been a little more room it might not have happened.

I thought, I can't believe this!

Fortunately, I had a mattress repair kit, which I gave to him. Despite the damage being in a bad position, right on a seam where the glue had melted from the heat, Geoff set about repairing his mattress. The mood went quiet. No one said anything. We just waited quietly to find out if the repairs worked. Or not.

From that point on I accepted whatever space was going.

As it happened, the repairs worked for the rest of the trip.

## SUNDAY, DECEMBER 7, 2003

We woke later than usual, despite shaking down to a pattern, aiming to set off on our journey each day at 7 o'clock in the evening. First thing was to go for a pee, then breakfast, including at least two drinks, after which we hoped to be able to walk off on our own for the daily constitutional. I considered it important to have a constitutional at the right time of the day, for my body to work like a clock. Astonishingly, it did so, and I was relieved each time it happened, though there were two or three occasions later when my body went out of kilter. I went out to dig a hole, and because I did not want to be out there for long, not being fully clothed, I wore the fewest clothes that I could get away with for the shortest period of time.

I had told Geoff that one of my problems in Greenland was that the wind caused problems with my toilet paper. He advised me to prepare the paper before I left the tent; for some reason that had never occurred to me. As we did not wake or eat breakfast at the same time, by the time Ronny ate his breakfast, I was preparing my toilet wad, folding it so I could reduce the amount of time I was out there. I felt embarrassed about this, sitting next to him, shoulder to shoulder, but he seemed unconcerned.

Ronny may have stayed in his sleeping bag longer than Geoff and I, not just because he was so much younger, but also to relieve the stress he felt in the middle of the tent. He later admitted to fearing that he might knock over things on both sides of him. On one side was my drink, on the other the stove. At least Geoff and I had one side that was safe, while Ronny felt confined in a virtual strait jacket in the middle.

He might have sought solace in music on a personal CD player, but we had immediately banned that. He had an audio system with him, but Geoff did not approve; neither did I. Ronny wanted to sit in the tent with his CD player leads in his ears, but I thought this was anti-social. He had taken his CD player out the first day, and it was like, "when are you going to use that! We don't like them." I told him that even on a modern-day train journey, if someone sat next to me with one of those things playing, I told them to turn it off. One of the reasons I did not travel on trains any more was that I could not stand people who travelled playing their personal stereos. Ronny's stereo was good quality and we were not able to hear it even close up.

Actually, we did not say we did not want him to use it. What both Geoff and I said was that we disapproved of the type of people who used them. We obviously did not know about Ronny using the system if he was half a mile away from us. But even if we did know about it, neither Geoff nor I liked it. Perhaps it was a generational thing.

After breakfast and a constitutional I would go back inside the tent and prepare my clothing. Geoff had cooked and I was only occasionally involved in washing up. It was not cold in the tent, but with washing up, something I would not want to admit to the family at home was that we used toilet paper to dry things.

Breaking up camp and preparing everything to leave took about half an hour. I looked after my own equipment, and shared responsibility for some provisions. Only one person could carry the tent, but everything else was shared. All the sledges weighed the same.

There was more enthusiasm to get on the trail when the wind was good. If the wind was poor we dawdled and hoped the wind would improve.

The day proved to be tough, in which I again fell continuously and bruised every bone in my body. On the previous two times I had used the kite I had not travelled very far at all. Now I was kiting for the third day, and having to put a lot of effort into keeping up. It was my first prolonged experience of kiting, but

I covered much more ground than on our previous kiting periods, five miles, despite a lot of falling over. There was a great deal of swearing and a lot of anger, but of course no one could hear because they were a long way away. The anger was not directed at either of my companions. It was mainly frustration with myself, that I was still not doing it properly.

Fortunately, the wind crept up in strength, and for the rest of the day we were able to use sails. I felt the first injuries coming on, minor body ailments, mainly from falling over. With the strain from being pulled by the kite, my neck became sore and my left foot had a swelling on the bone. When we moved from kite to sail, I was able to use the 14 square metres, the big one, and we were able to get some miles in. Having done 5 miles in 4 hours with kites, we changed to sails and over the next 5 hours we were able to do another 24 miles. That meant we had travelled in that period at nearly 5 miles an hour, pretty fast, making it a big day. I felt we had made a significant step that day, with a daily distance of 29.2 miles.

I was never the weakest member on a sail. Typically, Ronny, the expert at both types of travelling, had the ability to lead all the time, but I think out of good manners did not do so. He allowed either Geoff or myself to lead. I think he always felt he could be of greater assistance if he hung around in the middle or trailed at the back, in case of trouble.

We had dropped only 400 feet in four day's travelling, over an accumulated distance of 74 miles, so we were still at 9,000 feet, still capable at this height of suffering altitude sickness. I was not suffering, but I kept my tablets in my top pocket.

Setting up camp that evening, Geoff went in to cook, I dug walls around the tent as protection, while Ronny went for ice to melt to cook with. I had a deliberate reason for being the last into the tent. I did not want to be seen as the first one diving into the tent, and the *faux pas* over the demand for a three-inch gap still stung. It would take me longer to fold up the kite, or to sort out my bags outside and prepare for the morning, to ensure I was always last in.

Everything we carried was in one bag or another. It was bags and bags, except for the tent. Every single thing went into a bag, and that bag went into another bag. Geoff wrote in his diary a whole section about bags. He claimed it was a question of choosing which bags went to the bottom of the sledge, and which did not. Some of the bags were numbered, some coloured. The sails were a big part of the bulk of the sledge. Which were we going to use, and which would not be suitable that day? We were not able to fall into a routine, because things changed daily, depending on conditions.

With the three sails and the kite, they all went to the back of the sledge. Each needed to be easily accessible.

I bought North Face bags because I thought they were the best. They were expedition bags and they had great big zips on them. But a day before I left for the Antarctic I needed another bag, and I could not get the North Face bag I wanted. I rang a shop and the assistant there said he had Berghaus bags and claimed they were better than North Face. He made such a strong case that I drove to his shop, 20 miles away, and bought a Berghaus even though part of me was sceptical about his opinion. I needed the extra bag, and indeed, the Berghaus was so much better. In extremely cold conditions the North Face bag became brittle, and the zip was difficult to work. Instead of it being flexible, it was difficult to undo or do up, even though built for the cold. With the Berghaus I never had a problem, and in the future I would choose a Berghaus for extreme cold conditions.

I had two North Face bags, which I had bought because I had seen other people using them. North Face was American, and I think Berghaus, despite its name, was British. I naturally assumed that North Face bags would be as good as their other equipment, because they were top quality outfitters. But they had become so big in America people believe that they were now buying stuff from China. It was not the same quality.

On the timing of entering the tent, Geoff said later he always felt guilty about going into the tent first, as the first one to get into the protective warmth. He had to go into the tent first to start the cooking, but he felt that by doing it every day, he was having it easy. But though I was trying not to hang around outside doing nothing, once Ronny went in and I had calculated he had had enough time to take his boots off, then I could safely enter. Moving around, shifting clothes, there was not room for three of us to do this at the same time.

I looked after my minor ailments, putting cream on the bone that was beginning to be very sore. I tried to protect what I could, even though there was not much I could do.

In the night it was windy. We went to sleep with high hopes of a big day ahead, after the best part of 30 miles on the plateau that day, well above our average. Everything was looking good. We were so reliant on the wind; it was a dominant part of our life. When it was windy at night, even though it sometimes prevented me from getting to sleep easily, I often thought, we had 24 hours of daylight, there was wind out there, what were we doing lying in bed?

We could be on the trail still!

Geoff, much more experienced than me, had a different view. He did not think we should "chase the wind", because we could easily wear ourselves out whenever it was there. He felt we should fall into a pattern, take our calories, have our rests, and there was no long term point, after having done a day's work, in going out immediately to do another's day's work, just to catch the wind.

We had, from the beginning, conformed to what Geoff called the "5 o'clock Rule". He asked Ronny and me to stick to it, that we would always stop travelling at 5 o'clock in the morning, even if the wind was good. There were to be exceptions, but that was the rule. Ronny bought into it too, despite being the youngest of us, and able to go on skiing, though initially he did not see the value or discipline in it. This was where Geoff's Antarctic expedition experience counted. There was a difference between doing a weekly ski trip, which was what Ronny did in Norway, and a longer expedition. Geoff felt we needed to look after our bodies in a different way, and not take needless risks. There were disciplines that Geoff brought to the party that were necessary to complete a successful trip. The 5 o'clock rule was one of them.

There were times when I woke up in the middle of the night, and it was so good with a clean wind blowing in the right direction, and I just wished the other two were awake at that moment and one of them said, shall we go?

If they did, we would be gone!

That night, though, I listened to the wind and thought fruitless thoughts.

## MONDAY, DECEMBER 8, 2003

When we woke the following day, the wind had died.

It was a real choker.

We had breakfast and packed camp, but we could not go anywhere without a wind to help us. In that early part of the trip I still thought, if I had been on my own, I would have gone on the previous evening while there was wind. Being reliant on the weather, we could never know whether we will get wind the following day. I thought we should take it when it was there. But with three of us, consensus ruled. Geoff had the most experience of Antarctic travel.

One part of me accepted that he was right, because at the end of a working day we were all tired, even if the wind remained blowing. I knew we could not be taking chances with accidents, and starting again without a good night's sleep could cause accidents to happen. It was not going to be in my interests, or anyone's interests, to have an accident. Geoff pressed us to control our desire to carry on travelling when there was wind. Had it been left to Ronny and me, we would have cut corners.

It can be argued later that the fact that we survived the expedition meant that Geoff was right. I never teased Geoff about anything, but I may have put unintentional pressure on him. I had not intended to put pressure on him, but I was struggling to understand myself what was the right thing to do.

After all that wishful thinking during the windy night, we travelled just a third of a nautical mile in the whole day. We moved first thing in the morning and then just did not move at all. It was a great day for rest, because only the previous day I had started to show a few ailments. I had had a really tough kiting day, my foot was hurting. I knew that we were not going to do big distances every day.

I spent much of the day reading "The Beckoning Silence" by the great climber, Joe Simpson. We all read, retreating into our own little world composed of other people's words. We had plenty to drink, more drinks than we normally had, but we could only eat the food that had been allocated to that day. The tent was warm; outside, the temperature was minus 27.

I continued to collect thoughts. Ronny, I wrote, was a gem in the field and not a problem in the tent. He had been a real team-member in the skiing, and had a similar attitude in the tent. He was in the middle, accommodating, and a good chap.

It was apparent that Geoff was a Marmite freak. He had the traditional qualities of an English schoolboy, and like other boys at public school, he had his private stock of Marmite. For our journey, rather than taking a full jar, he had filled three film capsules with Marmite. This was over and above our normal provisions, Geoff's little luxury, and it was clearly a treat each day that Geoff looked forward to. But as we shared the tent, so Geoff offered to share his Marmite with us. I did eat some of it, even knowing how much Geoff loved it, but there was not going to be enough for many days if we all had some. Ronny, a Norwegian not brought up as a Marmite baby, needed to be told by Geoff that he did not require a lot of Marmite on his biscuit to taste it, that a scraping was enough. Ronny had never eaten Marmite before and did not know how much or how little was needed. He said that he really liked it (we subsequently sent him some Marmite to Norway).

The only private stock of food I had was a large bar of chocolate, but we had so much chocolate anyway, much more than I had realised when we were gathering together our provisions. Ronny did not have his own private food store, and came to a similar conclusion to me about not taking the Marmite on offer after having taken it once. Geoff continued to offer it to us and we continued to turn it down, but that was not because we did not want to eat it.

That evening I raised the issue of whether we should have carried on beyond our normal time, while the wind was blowing.

"We didn't go and now we can't go," I said, "because there's no wind. But there was a wind which we wasted because we slept."

But Geoff convinced me that the pattern he insisted on was best for the Antarctic. It was an issue that would come back to haunt us.

That day was just a day of rest.

# 9

## Tuesday, December 9, 2003

I woke up at 1330, and the wind was blowing again!

This was at least five hours ahead of our normal leaving time, and I lay there, frustrated. We had not moved the day before, we were well rested, and I had slept enough. There was loads of wind outside, it was 24-hour daylight, and I wanted to wake the others up and go.

Even though Geoff had convinced me the previous day of the merits of a 24-hour a day routine, I wanted to break that routine. I did it in an odd way. One of the things I took with me was an electric razor. Misha had told me that he did not believe in people having beards in Polar Regions. They were, he said, not necessary, and it was better to have a clean face and not have the snow blowing and sticking to your face, which made you even colder. People who had beards, he claimed, did it for effect, and professionals did not have beards.

Ronny always had a beard throughout his life, though he did reduce it on our expedition, but Geoff shaved as well. Yet Geoff thought the only way one could shave on an expedition was by a cold shave. He had been very sceptical about me turning up with an electric razor with a couple of double-A batteries that, he thought, would not last five minutes. Geoff said, "I can't believe you've brought that", because he thought that was not a sensible thing to have done. But I had managed to keep a razor going in Greenland, and we had plenty of batteries, and I felt that I could keep the electric razor going.

I found myself contemplating using the noise of the electric razor as a means of getting my way. Bursting to wake them up yet restrained by custom and practice in tent behaviour, I hummed and hawed in my sleeping bag.

After about half an hour, I started to shave.

"It's a bit early to shave, isn't it?" said Geoff, sleepily, waking at the noise.

"Probably," I said, "sorry, probably is, but actually have you noticed how good the weather is?"

It was not a successful ploy.

Ronny wanted to stay in bed, and Geoff wanted his eight hours. I lay there half-awake and half asleep, not tired at all, desperate to go. I felt a bit guilty about the razor trick, but I wanted to see if we could reach a consensus that we should get out immediately. Another hour went by before there was any surfacing of individuals. We did leave fifty minutes earlier than we normally left, starting at 1810 local instead of 1900.

I felt particularly upbeat, having recovered from the slight strains of the body during the previous day's rest. The wind was sufficient that we could get away with sails. Mentally I had allowed for four days for non-travelling (I do not know why I came up with the figure 4). Out of six days of food, we had one day acclimatising at the Pole, one day in the tent, so we had actually only travelled on four days out of the six, and we had done 74 miles. This was below the average daily mileage I was looking for (20 miles/day), but with a good wind, we could now make some good progress.

While the wind was good, visibility was poor. That made it a tough day. Travelling fast with poor visibility, I could not see the *sastrugi*, which I kept hitting. I would avoid some of it and then ski straight into the next piece. This put a degree of strain on my legs, having to ski over more *sastrugi* than I wanted to, and not being totally balanced. When I could see the *sastrugi* I kept my balance better. All three of us were frustrated at our sledges over-turning.

When I travelled, I travelled fast, but my actual performance on the hour was poor because of the number of times I had to stop to turn my sledge back upright.

It was not physically difficult, just a constant frustration. There were times when I became separated from my partners, which added to my stress. I knew that if we had clear good conditions, it did not normally go from clear to whiteout immediately. But if we already had poor conditions, we could hit a whiteout instantaneously. I was nervous about being as separated as we sometimes were. Whoever was skiing first navigated, having agreed at the beginning of the day which direction to take. We knew we had to monitor our course throughout the day, because we normally navigated by the sun. But if there was no sun, we would ski over an angle to the blown *sastrugi*, because the *sastrugi* was always ridged in the same direction, and we maintained a constant angle to it.

We all had GPS's, and were constantly taking a position as to how many degrees west we were. Obviously, we stopped from time to time to see how far we had travelled. That was one of the little joys of the journey, travelling and then waiting for other team members, and first thing I would do is pull out my GPS and see how far I had travelled. At the same time I would check I was travelling the right longitude.

There was a fair degree of waiting on the whole trip. There was never a time where we could go an hour without having to stop and wait. The faster we travelled, the more we had to stop. If I lost contact with one of the team, I was more likely to do it when travelling well.

This was irritating whether it was me being left behind or whether I was ahead and waiting. If I was left behind I could not understand why it was my sledge that was going over all the time. It took longer to correct the sledge when I was using a kite with lines of 50 metres, than if I had to correct a sledge with a sail which had lines only 5 metres long.

With a kite I had to bring it down, control it with the wind blowing, and not allow it to get caught up in *sastrugi*. Then I could turn the sledge upright again. Bringing the kite down in slightly windy conditions because my sledge had fallen over was not hazardous, but what could be a simple flick of a sledge could result in five or ten minutes delay. I knew that if I had two over-turns, and my partners did not have a sledge turned over, they were going to be out of sight.

Strange things happened to my mind.

If I was suffering sledge over-turns, I consciously wanted the others to suffer too. If that happened, I felt, then we were sharing the holding up together. There were two typical times when I wanted someone else's sledge to go over. Either I wanted to have a rest, or we were not going to have a rest until the sledge fell over. But if someone was going out of sight ahead of me and I was still rolling my sledge back over again, there were times when I fiercely thought, I hope his sledge falls over in a minute. I thought it was weird to have such thoughts, that I actually would really like someone else's sledge to fall over. The mere fact that I thought this distressed me; it seemed a bit selfish.

Geoff always kept his cards very close to his chest as to what he thought about matters like this. He never expressed an opinion on these matters.

Of course, there were other times when I prayed that no one's sledge went over. That was when I was a long way in front, it was cold, and the wind was blowing. When someone else's sledge kept falling over and I was getting cold waiting for him, I really wanted his sledge to behave. And yet, maybe half an hour earlier I had been wishing it to fall over. Both sentiments were felt strongly, but one seemed to be more honourable than the other.

We constantly watched each other. It was easier to watch people if they were side by side, or in front of me. If I was going well, I was so grateful, and it was difficult to look around and see where my companions were behind me.

Visually, we were out of touch more times that day than we should have been. We had no artificial aids like radios. I think we were aware that losing touch with each other was not something we should be doing, and tried our best to restrict the times that it happened. But inevitably on a journey like this, that happened. There was no way of telling someone if I was just ten feet behind them, unless they looked back. If I was close to someone and my sledge went over, they would not actually know that it had fallen over for some time. It depended how often they slowed down to see if their partners were there.

That particular day, we travelled 36.9 miles, the best distance so far. The weather improved enough for me to take video pictures, the first time that I had used the video camera. Because we had started early we finished and camped half an hour earlier than usual.

We added up the accumulated total, 111 miles in 7 days. That was acceptable.

Yet that evening I made notes about how fragile the balance was between life and death. We were still on a plateau, still at 9,000 feet, and we had gone several days where, if we had needed an aircraft to rescue us, none could have landed because the *sastrugi* was bigger than it normally was. I knew that each time I fell, then if I did hurt myself, that would be serious. I was acutely aware of our isolation.

We knew at that point there would not be an easy rescue, if one were necessary, either for myself or for my companions. From my position, I cared more about them. If something happened to me, well, that was my fault. But if something happened to one of the others on an expedition that I had initiated, it would have ruined my journey. I was scared of something happening to them as much as I was scared for myself.

By now my sledge and Ronny's sledge, despite being made of Kevlar, had started to crack, and needed repairing. Geoff had a lot of rope with him. I was shown how to sew up the sides of the sledge, stitching with rope. We also had run out of spare Pulk arms, metal arms for the sledge to attach to the harness. We had brought two spares, but within seven days of skiing had used them both. We had spare nuts, used for attaching the Pulk arms to the harness, and started using those, but they were wearing through, the metal breaking from the constant rattling and jarring. Geoff started hooking his rope into his harness. Of course the rope had a short longevity, and that caused an additional problem. It was the stress of the conditions, the high *sastrugi* we had to sail over at speed with the kites and sail that took its toll. If we had been walking, it would not have had the same effect.

I used a plastic drinking bottle to enable me to pee in the middle of the night without leaving my sleeping bags. On paper, these were unbreakable. Geoff also used one, but conditions had become so bad that when we unloaded the battered sledges, Geoff found his pee-bottle had broken. I never dreamt these bottles could break. Ronny, who slept in the middle, had never felt com-

*Sometimes a rolled sledge took us completely off our skis.* ©*Ronny Finsaas*

*Above and following – Beautiful examples of sastrugi encountered on our journey.   © Ronny Finsaas*

fortable about using his bottle for a pee, and he always got out of the tent instead. That meant there was a spare pee bottle available for Geoff.

I used my pee bottle a lot. After that, instead of just throwing the empty bottle into the bag when I was packing up, I was more careful about how I packed it.

## WEDNESDAY, DECEMBER 10, 2003

The frustration on the eighth day was that it was the first time the weather came from the north. Weather normally came up from the south. Having a weather system bringing a front from the sea to the north that far inland was not common, high up on the plateau. Two changes had to happen for us to make progress, not just one. Visibility was poor, and even if the wind had been in the right direction we would not have been able to travel.

There was also some snow. I had always understood Antarctica to have little snow, and it did not snow very much, but it snowed that day, and from the north.

We had nothing to do but sit in a tent, our second non-travelling day. We were still at altitude, with occasional shortness of breath and needing to drink a lot. Periods like this were about mental control. We were constantly calculating – and believing – that if we could get 150 miles from the Pole, we would then start to lose height, the wind would gather speed off the ice, and when we got past the halfway distance our progress would speed up. Having that belief was important. We needed not to panic while we were hunkered down, and keep believing we could get those extra miles done.

## THURSDAY, DECEMBER 11, 2003

A second consecutive day of doing nothing, the weather still coming in from the north. It was not particularly comfortable in the cramped tent, and better to get out and go for a walk. We did that. There was a lot of conversation, but we read a lot too, in the 24 hours of daylight. We did not play any cards, any team games, but we shared books.

Ronny, very much a do-er, accustomed to getting out every morning and going skiing in Norway, once showed his frustration. He was irritated at the delays. I was feeling the same way, except I would never have expressed this feeling. Sure enough Geoff rebuked him quickly, saying the situation we were in was nothing. Geoff said this was only our third day of delay out of nine. While working for the British Antarctic Survey, he recalled having to spend 60 days waiting for an aircraft to pick him up. Ronny was firmly put in his place about a mere three-day delay. I was pleased that it had not been me that had expressed any frustration, even though I felt it.

I wondered about the ethics of ski sailing that were increasingly governing my behaviour when we were travelling. It was sometimes acceptable, for example, to follow the tracks of the other two, but other times I thought I should not do it. A lot of the time I enjoyed being out in front, which was not a problem if we were using sail. But I was often last on kiting days, and more than with the other two, my sledge kept falling over. I could not understand why someone else was not having this problem. I did think that if I could follow their tracks, then maybe my sledge would not roll over either. But as soon as I started following someone else's tracks, I felt that with all this open space, the idea that I was not even cutting my own trail was cheating. I was allowing someone else to carve out my journey, and I resisted this.

I did not know how the other two felt, because I did not ask them. We were going in the same direction and following each other. Being within ten to twenty feet of someone else's tracks was acceptable, because there were times we wanted to stay as close as possible. It was, in part, an aesthetic decision. Having been a recreational skier for years, there was nothing more pleasurable than carving new ski-tracks in the snow. In the Antarctic, with all the choice in the world to do that, why should I want to follow exactly where someone else had skied? To answer that it may mean my sledge turning over less often was not enough. It meant, in my mind, when I did it to avoid my sledge falling over, it was being clever. But when I thought I was cheating, it was a dilemma, which I did not enjoy.

I also thought that day that one of the principal reasons for making the journey in the first place was to discover how I could cope with setbacks. In some ways, the fact that we were so well prepared meant we did not have as many setbacks as I had expected. Mentally, I was worried that I would not be as tested as I had thought I might be. This was not just a physical journey. I chose the location, in the extreme cold and isolation, to see how well I could cope.

I felt that I had to have a poker player's skills, handling the appearance of any emotion.

It may not have been a factor for the other two. They may not have considered it so important. For me it was important to have a poker face, whether it was going well or badly.

I think I felt that if I was under extreme pressure and if I showed emotion, then that was a weakness.

Geoff was a consummate professional, but it was actually pleasing to me to see him raging with anger at his sledge one day. He probably thought it was happening out of sight of the rest of us. I am sure that if I had asked him about it, he would not have admitted getting angry.

## FRIDAY, DECEMBER 12, 2003

We woke to a day of good visibility and a northeast wind, but there were other problems. The sledges continued to deteriorate, and the previous day's dinner did not agree with me. I had to make two unscheduled stops.

I was beginning to think the food selection could have been better. Every day there would be a cheer about what came out of the food bag, but we had too many curries. Geoff had bought the main meals from Canada, all freeze-dried. I think he had gone down the line and had not looked at the ingredients, just took a selection of all that they had.

One of the curries was disagreeable for all of us. Only wanting one constitutional a day, the idea of having three was a real pain, because it meant more delays. I got left behind, and suffered miserably from the cold. It was a long process getting my clothes off and then getting them back on again, including in and out of my harness and Pulks. I was prepared for it, but it did not make it any easier.

Geoff also struggled. It was a day when we had to start with our largest sail, which meant the wind was not great. I found myself leading the group, which meant I had to drop my sail often. Ronny travelled between Geoff and me, and we did our first 20 miles in good time. The wind picked up, and I dropped down to the 10 SqM sail, but the wind gusted stronger, and Geoff wanted to go down to the 5 SqM sail.

This was, I felt, undergearing the sail, more than I felt was appropriate.

I seemed to be able to cope with sailing with gusty winds, though on this day I had a problem. It happened when I had the sail on the ground, and I normally pulled it up while it was not attached to me. If it had been ruffled up, I would pick it up by its lines and sort it out in the wind, so that when it blew open and worked properly, I was able to click it into my harness. But if the wind gusted during this process, I just did not have the strength in my arms to hold it, and it would be snatched away.

It was the only time on the trip this happened to me; just as I was about to click in, the wind gusted and the sail was taken from me. I could not chase it because I was attached to my sledge. Ronny already had his sail up, and he went after my sail. He did not have far to go because the sail was caught up in the *sastrugi*. Had it been a smooth surface, the sail could have travelled for miles like a riderless horse.

Geoff did not have a lot of experience using sails, and tried to control them by holding the rope instead of holding the bar. That meant he did not have the same level of control as Ronny and me. The right way to hold a sail was with the right hand at the top of the bar, controlling everything from there, but because Geoff did not grip his sail properly, he often opted in high winds to go to smaller sails than were necessary.

Not holding the control bar correctly irritated me. I did not have a problem with him not having a lot of experience, but why did he not hold the sail correctly?

But there was another problem that had been building up inside me all that day, exacerbated by the increasing damage to our sledges. It was about buying them second-hand. This problem had not been totally confronted as the sledges started to break, and now Ronny's and mine became quite badly damaged.

When I first saw the sledges were damaged, I recalled my frustration that I had sent money to Geoff in September to buy new sledges. I had agreed a price for all of the provisions, including his salary and expenses for preparing the trip, the flights, everything built into one budget. The price included $2,000 each for three new sledges, in a total budget that came to more than $200,000. A few weeks later, in October, Geoff had told me he had managed to get some very good sledges, but they were second hand. They were, he said, as good as new, having had one short and easy journey in the Arctic. I had been irritated, but I moved on.

Then the sledges broke and I was furious.

I was furious because, if we had had new sledges, maybe they would not have broken? Yet it did not matter if new ones would have broken or would not have broken. I had spent a couple of hundred thousand dollars on the trip, and everything had been new – sails, kites, and skis – everything except for the sledges. The idea of saving perhaps $3,000 – say the second-hand sledges were half price – could be the difference between the trip being successful or failing.

With nothing else to think about all day, this issue stewed inside me, but I bided my time. As the day went on and the damage to the sledges increased, it became a bigger and bigger issue for me. There were not a lot of other things to think about, except the journey we were doing. Hour after hour of struggling went by, as the sledges fell into a seriously damaged state, while I brooded that maybe this would be the one thing that would prevent me from achieving my goal.

I vented my frustration that evening.

"Tell me again why we had to have the second-hand sledges?" I asked Geoff.

He had explained at the time that it was going to take six weeks to build new sledges, and add to that the time afterwards for delivery. Factor into this, he said again patiently that evening, the way the trip was put together after the delays, with ANI dropping out and Mike Sharp cobbling together the whole business. Then add in my late commitment in mid-September. By the time I got the cheque to him to buy the sledges in the third week in September, Geoff said, along with him having to go down to Antarctica to support Rosie Stancer in early November; there just had not been enough time to get new sledges. He said he was fortunate to get the sledges he did buy, which in his opinion were as good as new anyway. There was no way he would have attempted to do the trip in sledges that were not good enough.

I had authorised Geoff to buy Kevlar sledges, and the second-hand sledges we had were made of Kevlar, the toughest material available and not the more fragile and cheaper fibreglass. It was Geoff's opinion that even if we had bought new sledges they would have suffered similar damage, even though Kevlar could be mended where fibreglass could not. So we had the same sledges as we would have had if they were new.

Geoff's explanation was quite legitimate, and I found it acceptable. But in my own mind, I was not able to come to terms with it for two or three days. It rankled with me for that length of time, that we were using second-hand sledges.

In this conversation, which I noted in my diary as a "small discussion" in the tent, Ronny was left sitting in the middle. He said and did nothing. It was always a full and frank discussion, when we aired our views, but Ronny was not involved in this issue.

Though we had a brilliant day's travelling, covering 45 miles, the backs of the sledges were now broken. We had good winds and we had skied for 11 hours, but the bottom halves of the sledges had splits in them. They were letting in snow, collecting it as we went along, piling it into the sledge.

*Coping with the disintegrating sledges covered a number of days, and involved some complicated trading.*

*We had to spend three hours on the morning of December 13 sewing the sledges up like patchwork with a drill and rope. Their integrity was deteriorating as they lost the shape of their bodies, and despite our repairs they continued to deteriorate. Geoff did the majority of the mending. He had spares that we used to pull the sledges together, though Ronny had back-up spares too.*

*I rang Mike Sharp at Patriot Hills on the satellite phone, to ask for replacement sledges. At that stage I just wanted to know if any were available, no more than that. Geoff was of the opinion that perhaps we could get through the complete journey on our current sledges. Conditions were bound to improve once off the plateau, he thought, and if we had to he could get them home to complete the journey, despite the damage. I was especially keen not to change my sledge, because the one I was using had my coat of arms* on it, and I wanted this coat of arms to go all the way with me from the Pole to Hercules Inlet. I wanted to believe it when Geoff said he was confident that, however badly damaged they were, he would get them home. But there were other matters at stake.

Clearly we had a serious problem. We had to alert base camp to it, because it could cause the trip to end early. We did not know the trail conditions we were due to confront. They might improve, especially the surfaces, which would do less damage to the sledges, but we did not know for certain that they would.

In the middle of my phone conversation to Mike Sharp, Geoff suddenly said: "I know there are at least three sledges in the ice cave at base camp!"

These had been used several times before, so they were also not new, and add to that, they were made of fibreglass. But at that time, I was keen on anything that would enable us to complete the trip.

First I had to establish whether they were there. Then, a crucial question this, would Mike be prepared to bring them into Thiel Mountains, the halfway distance on our journey? We were still some way off Thiel, with another 150 miles to go. It had taken us 10 days to cover 180 miles. I did another calculation; we had used 11 food days, skiing on only 7 of them. To cover the remaining distance, 427 miles, we had 19 day's food left, and more than two-thirds of our journey still to do. At that rate, we were going to be out of food before we finished.

Yet we had to assume conditions would get better. We were still behind our schedule, but we had expected the first few days to travel slowly. Having the damaged sledges was slowing us up. When they rolled over, without their normal integrity they were more difficult to turn back again.

The following day, a deal was worked out.

Mike said he could supply sledges at Thiel Mountains. Independently, Patriot Hills asked Ronny if he was prepared to stay on for a professional job, taking a couple of weeks to teach a Malaysian girl to ski sail in Antarctica. Ronny said he wanted to complete the journey with Geoff and me first, but after that he was happy to do this job. I said that Ronny and the Malaysian girl could use my sails and kites.

Mike suggested the quid pro quo, and I needed it to come from Mike than from me. I had signed a contract agreeing that if I needed the Twin Otter to re-supply me, it was going to cost US$19,500/hour. It would be a five-hour flight from Patriot Hills to Thiel and back, so the cost could be close to a hundred thousand dollars. I would have found that an excessive expense, because I knew they did runs into Thiel anyway, and I had asked Mike to piggyback the sledges on a regular fuel trip. Mike said he would do the piggyback operation. The loan of the fibreglass sledges, which is what it was, was a quid pro quo for the loan of my equipment, the sails and kites to teach the Malaysian girl. I presumed he came to a cash deal with her.

Sitting in a tent, totally isolated and in desperate need, I did not have many high cards. But I thought my friendship with Mike Sharp, and my role, however slight, in enabling him to set up in business that year, was good enough to make this deal work. There was good will there. Nevertheless, the good will had to come from Mike, rather than me asking for it.

## SATURDAY, DECEMBER 13, 2003

As if the sledge business was not enough, tensions grew between Geoff and me that day about choosing which size sail to use.

Changing sails and kites was always a matter of judgement and timing. It was a judgement between safety and speed. Geoff saw the changing of sails and kites as a big decision, every time it was taken. If we got it wrong, we wasted a lot of time. With kites, it could take half an hour, though with sails, perhaps ten minutes.

There were times when we all agreed it was appropriate to change. But there were times when one of us unilaterally wanted to change, and this put pressure on the other two to change as well. If it was not felt to be the right decision, there were tensions – "Can't we keep going? Can't we just ride out the current situation?" – but Geoff always thought of safety first.

He wanted minimal risk.

Much of the time I did not agree with the changing of the sail, usually down to a smaller and slower but safer size. Obviously there were times when he was right to make that decision. If the wind picked up and we had stayed with the bigger sail, it would have been risky. But there were times when a decision to downsize was taken, and it was a wrong decision. Geoff could always say all the decisions taken were the right ones, because the trek ended successfully. But at the time there were tensions when Geoff chose to change the sail when we could have happily continued as we were.

I was constantly having a problem with cold hands, despite having five or six pairs of gloves, and the means to get four pairs of gloves on at the same time. It was a real struggle to keep my hands warm. There were so many times when I could have used charcoal hand-warmers.

(The irony was, I had packed them, but forgotten that I had them with me. I had picked them up in a shop, thinking I would never need them because my glove system was too good, and anyway they would not work. My mind was so focussed all the way through, that mentally I never bought into the fact that I actually had them. It was not until I unpacked at base camp when it was all over that I found them in my bag. I thought, "bloody hell, I had hand warmers!")

When my hands were really cold, I used some down mitts made by Rab – the clothes manufacturer – extra-large expedition mitts that allowed other gloves to go inside them. This was not necessary, because the mitts were most efficient when worn on their own, but I could not wear them all the time because they were difficult to work with. It was not just the 30 degrees below zero but also the wind that froze my hands. Controlling the sail or kite, my hands were upside down and in the air, the blood draining out of them. Holding the control bar stopped circulation, and made it more difficult to keep them warm. When everything else failed, every different combination of gloves, even though I could not work with the down mitts, I knew I would never have frost-bitten hands because I had them in reserve.

That day, December 13, despite the problems with the sledges and the three hours work to repair them before travelling, we did 25 miles. This was better than the average we needed, but Geoff struggled using the biggest sail, the 14 SqM, the next sail up from a kite.

## SUNDAY, DECEMBER 14, 2003

We did 28.5 miles, much of it with a kite!

By this time, skiing with a kite was beginning to make sense to me. It was my big day with it, the best I had done. After this I considered I was never the weakest member with the kite, so long as some wind was blowing. When there was hardly any wind my technique was exposed, but as soon as there was a bit of wind to work with, I could hold my own.

We were now repairing the sledges every morning. It was an additional irritation, especially as it stopped us taking advantage of good conditions. But in another way, it was proving to be one of those obstacles that added to the achievement. The repairs were difficulties that had to be overcome, and there was something satisfying about completing the trip with broken sledges.

For a while, I dreamt that it was possible to get to the end by continuing to repair the Kevlar sledges. The problem with that reasoning was that Mike Sharp had already made us an offer of fibreglass sledges. He was planning to drop them into the cache at Thiel Mountains on his next fuel trip, which had been delayed. That offer was there with no cost to me. As much as I wanted to continue with the existing sledges, I could only be criticised if I had turned the offer down. If we continued with our original broken sledges and then failed, and needed to be rescued, I faced real criticism. There was no up-side in turning down the offer of the sledges. It had to be a pragmatic decision to say we would take them, even though I did it with a heavy heart.

I knew it was sentimental to cherish a broken sledge because of a coat of arms, but that was how I felt. I wanted that sledge to be the one that I did my whole trip with, because I wanted to take that sledge home. I did not want to complete on another sledge.

By this time I had put behind me the rancour of having the second-hand sledges, for a simple logical reason.

*It had occurred to me, when Mike made the offer of the re-supply, that what was being offered were the original sledges that I was going to be using anyway!*

Had ANI kept going I would have been using those sledges, even though they were second-hand. I realised that was why I had not made any plans over the previous 2-½ years to buy any sledges, until I sent the cheque to Geoff at the end of September 2003.

*Because I had thought I had them already.*

Whatever irritation I felt that Geoff had bought second-hand sledges, I was also irritated with myself for having agreed to have second-hand sledges in the first place. I could not understand how, with all the planning I had put in, I had thoughtlessly signed off on everything that was going on, including ANI supplying me with second-hand sledges. They were very good sledges, but they were good *fibreglass* sledges, and Geoff had bought better Kevlar sledges.

Whether the fibreglass sledges would have broken up in the bad conditions that we had hit in the first week would be interesting to know.

## MONDAY, DECEMBER 15, 2003

We saw the world flight helicopter flown by Jennifer Murray and Colin Bodill pass us on its way back from the Pole to Patriot Hills. It circled us. We were in our sleeping bags, and we leant out of the tent and waved at them and took a picture (that was two days before they had the accident that ended the flight and nearly killed them both).

The rest of the day was disappointing, with very little distance covered, just 4.7 miles, because there was little wind. We needed to head east as well as north, and used a sail to begin with, but quickly changed to a kite. The sledges were OK going so slowly, and were not further damaged. We had had some more snow, and the *sastrugi* had flattened out. We got away and everything was looking good, and then suddenly the wind died and that was it.

After a while we made camp. I think that because we made camp early, Ronny got drafted in to do the cooking. It was my little joke with him.

"As we've got some time we'll have a gastronomic meal, Ronny, you can do it", I said.

He had few ingredients to work with, the same boil-in-the-bag food as Geoff cooked, but we wanted a gastronomic meal. The only real difference was that Ronny used three times the butter Geoff would have used.

Not being involved in preparation of food, at the same time as constantly receiving it, I thought I had been clever when I chose my position in the tent. Geoff had taken one side of the tent, I was allocated the middle and Ronny was on the other side. The cooker was going to be next to Geoff. I quickly suggested that Ronny should be in the middle and I should be at the other end of the tent from Geoff.

I had naturally assumed that, as they were the more experienced travellers, they would do the stove work, and indeed that proved to be the case. On one level I was pleased that I was not in the position to be able to do any cooking. There was no room for the stove to be anywhere near me, or indeed for me to get anywhere near the stove.

But then I thought, yet again, that I was always on the receiving end of things. I received my hot drink, I received my food, and I remember thinking that I was like the chick in the bird's nest waiting for the mother bird to feed me. I did not like that. Having thought it was clever not being next to the stove, I became guilty about being on the receiving end of the food.

I did not, however, feel guilty enough to ask to change places with Ronny, or to offer to cook.

They were doing great, there was no reason to replace them. The guilt was, I thought, something I felt I had to live with. Geoff did the majority of the cooking, and did not seem to have a problem with it. I never thought about asking him not to do it, or volunteer to do it myself. If I had suggested it, might he have felt he was not good enough?

That evening I heard about the advantages of using snow instead of toilet paper. We were talking about various camp conditions, and resources available to us on Polar expeditions. Geoff said that blocks of ice were very effective and much better than toilet paper. I thought I would go out and find blocks of ice and try it, despite having developed good techniques for folding toilet paper. Obviously, for cleanliness, a block of ice is effective, however uncomfortable. Once I got used to the sudden cold shock, ice was an added benefit.

I had also been suffering from cold feet, but noted that day that it was eased. It could have been the increase in the temperature that helped, or it could have been that each day I tried to alter the layers of socks on my feet in order to keep them warmer. Perhaps both reasons, including giving my feet a lot more room for movement, which enabled them to work and retain some heat. Geoff said he still had cold feet.

We were not downbeat that day about doing 4.7 miles. There was a sombre mood when our sledges broke, but other than that we remained upbeat for much of the journey. I did not think Ronny had ever seen broken sledges before, and he had not prepared for that. Geoff had never seen broken sledges either, and it made us all sombre.

Not long after I fell asleep, Geoff and Ronny woke me up. They said I was snoring. My snoring used to be quite bad, but having lost a lot of weight over the past few years I honestly believed it had improved. I had gone into a solid sleep and apparently started snoring. This was fair, I thought later, because they were being kept awake, but it crossed my mind whether I could actually have woken them if I had found them snoring. None of their sleeping habits was objectionable, but one of mine obviously was.

## TUESDAY, DECEMBER 16. 2003

The mindset of going into the day was that we had used 13 days' food. This included 4 days when we had achieved a total of 4.9miles; one day had been at the Pole, and we had had a full 8 days skiing, and completed one third of our trip. When we averaged that out, we contemplated facing 36 days on route, instead of the 30 days for which we had food. We knew that travelling conditions should improve, but also knew Antarctica would give us whatever weather it wanted to give us. When it gave us bad conditions, we had to accept them.

We wanted to change longitude 1-½ degrees east to avoid cravasses marked on the map (even though the map had them placed wrongly as we discovered later). To change longitude we needed to use sails, because tacking across the wind with a kite was difficult. If there was a following wind, then a kite was good if we were going in one direction. But if we wanted to get across a route by tacking, we needed to use sails.

When we looked out of the tent, the temperature had risen to minus 14, and there was not much wind. It was typical kiting weather. We left camp with little belief we could travel far. I got mine into the air and off I went, travelling over a surface that was noticeably easier. I was becoming pleased with my kiting because I was able to keep pace with the others and did not fall over once.

It was a confidence-building day, and enjoyable, but I got too close to Geoff at one point and my kite tangled with his. When we were kiting, until now Geoff was always in front and I was always some way behind him. But now I was able to hold my own kiting, so much so that I ran my kite across his kite, which was not particularly clever. He was not pleased after I had done that. Though he was not within earshot, I could tell by his body actions that he was asking, "why the hell are you so close to me?" We laughed about it later.

The wind was changeable, 10/12 knots, at the limit between the biggest sail and the kite. Nervous about it picking up, we reduced the length of line on the kites from 50 to 30 metres. The kite could be quite dangerous as a means of travelling, especially in high winds. A sail was not dangerous but a kite could be. There was a release mechanism to let the kite go, but if I did that I lost it, and I did not want to let it go. We only had one reserve kite.

With little friction from the good travelling surface, we were on the move for 6 hours before the wind faded. We had put 29.3 miles on the clock, the kind of target we had been looking for. We heard from Patriot Hills that the replacement sledges had not been dropped at Thiel Mountains. Our sledges were still deteriorating but the stitches were holding, as there was less surface battering. We saw Thiel Mountains for the first time, at best briefly. When we camped we still needed a real wind to get us 1-½ degrees east. Among my ailments, my foot bone was rubbing on the boot. Every day I was using heat cream on my foot, normally used on my back. It was helping.

I phoned my father. I knew that he would appreciate the call. It was the only time I called him, and I was obviously feeling positive (I would probably not have phoned if I had not felt positive). Dad was more concerned about what was happening than Mum was. I felt she could handle pressure better than he could. Obviously, I had little meaningful to say, sitting shoulder to shoulder with my two companions inside the tent.

# 10

# Wednesday, December 17, 2003

We left at 1900 for a really enjoyable morning. In 2 ½ hours, using kites, we did 11 miles. I now had sufficient experience with the kite to enjoy it, without all the early fears I had about falling over. There were still some nasty falls and I was pleased I was not injured, but that was a constant fear anyway. There were a couple of falls when I ended up a crumpled mess, head first down in the *sastrugi*.

On one occasion the sledge got caught on a pinnacle of *sastrugi* and could not ride over it. It stopped me, but the kite pulled me over headfirst into the rough surface. I was being pulled in one direction and the sledge was hooked in the ice. Something had to give, and for a while I thought it was me. We were not wearing helmets, though I was wearing a hat, and the *sastrugi* seemed large and full of hard ice. My body continued to ache.

There were phases at the beginning of the journey where I had ached, just getting into the routine of daily travelling. Then I went through a fit stage, and after two weeks on the go I was losing weight as the trip took its toll on my body. From this day on I felt a slight deterioration all the time, and was always concerned about a major injury. We needed to be physically fit, our bodies working in all parts to carry on.

The wind varied in strength, up and down, and we switched irregularly from kite to sail. We could see Thiel Mountains, which looked as if they were reachable, but at the end of the day they seemed just as far away.

It was a day of misunderstanding between the three of us. We had tried to get 1-½ degrees east the previous day, but failed. Ronny and I could see on the map that we needed to go further east, and we had the wind to do it. Ronny set off further east, but Geoff stayed on a direct course for Thiel. I was in the middle, not wanting to lose touch with either of them, Ronny on my right, Geoff on my left. There were times when one or the other would almost go out of sight. Clearly, I thought they could not possibly see each other because I could hardly see them myself. I wanted to follow Ronny because I knew what the map had indicated about crevasses, but I did not want to lose touch with Geoff. He seemed confident about what he was doing. It was a strenuous day. We did not resolve that situation until the end of the day, when we camped at the normal time of 5 o'clock in the morning. The wind picked up and we were all using sails, and we just seemed to come together, with them both converging on me. It had been quite a big day, and we were tired. The mountains seemed close at this stage.

Geoff told us that the direction Ronny and I had been trying to go had been too far east. We were trying to avoid crevasses marked on the map as close to the mountains, but it turned out the map was wrong. The map had also marked crevasses further east. The mountains were marked incorrectly, one whole degree out. Geoff, the experienced Antarctic traveller, knew he was on the right course, where Ronny and I had looked at the map at the beginning of the day and made different decisions.

Why did Geoff not get us to move over towards him?

He said he made some effort to join us and tell us, but every time he made that effort we went further east. In the end he decided to stay on the right course. He felt comfortable because he could see us, and conditions were reasonably good.

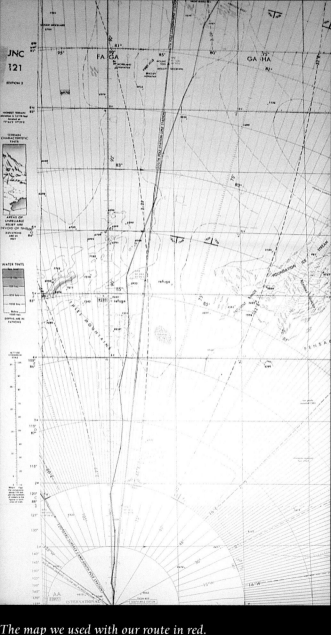

*The map we used with our route in red.*

*Geoff in the distance, waiting for Martin Burton.*

*Ronny with 14-sqm sail in good conditions.*

*Ronny working his arms hard using a kite.*

*Martin Burton (finally) enjoying his kite.*

*Best day of the journey, 51 nautical miles on Martin Burton's 50th birthday. Bunting supplied by Christina Burton via Geoff.*

*Final day on mountains above Hercules Inlet, only 15 miles to go.   © Geoff Somers*

*Ronny with a full sail.*  © *Geoff Somers*

I came to the conclusion that we had done two things wrong. One was that we had allowed too big a gap to exist between us. Geoff agreed that we should not allow that to happen again. The other was that, because Geoff did not like to eat during the day, we did not have a regular lunchtime stop, and Ronny and I picked at our food when we could. If other people had problems, I would eat. If I had problems, Ronny would eat. Geoff preferred to save his food and not eat during the day. Often Geoff might be near the front when we were kiting. I only had to have a bad day when my sledge was falling over, and by the time I caught up I had no time for a rest. Because Geoff did not eat, we did not need a fixed break and as soon as I got near him, he was off. He did not wait until I was alongside to talk to him, because of the 50 metre line kites and the risk of entanglement. As soon as I was within a hundred yards, Geoff turned and started travelling again. He knew I was well because I was travelling, so he felt there was no need to stop.

We sometimes skied two hours without a stop, at the end of which, all we did was create a bigger distance between us. If we did not stop, we got tired and had a greater risk of injury.

I told Geoff we needed to have some discipline on the way we were handling it, and build in a lunch break. He agreed to this, too.

A phone call to Mike Sharp confirmed he would get the sledges to us, but he was having other problems. All this time I had his commitment as an insurance policy, which meant I could continue with the original damaged sledges. Every time he said he could get the new sledges to us, paradoxically, I was not delighted about it. I was much happier knowing I could have them, than actually having them.

As we camped we were happy that the wind was picking up, though I had been pleased with my kiting. Geoff thought we might have skied over a number of crevasses. Our total distance travelled was 33 miles, which raised our averages, and we dropped below 5,000 feet for the first time, at 4,936 feet. Our cumulative distance travelled was 276 miles.

## THURSDAY, DECEMBER 18, 2003

For me it was important at all times to be second out of bed. I did not naturally like mornings, and could easily have been the last one to get up, but I made a point of this not happening. It was part, again, of not wanting to be the weakest member of the team, mentally or physically. I took it to the point where I could never be the last one out of bed. I knew that Geoff was an experienced Polar traveller, and Ronny was only 30 years of age and had been living in freezing conditions all his life. I just wanted to make sure I was a full member of the team, and did everything to ensure I was never holding anyone back. Getting up last had the potential to hold people back.

This little obsession created a problem I only found out about at the end of the journey. At the Pole, during discussions at the beginning of the month, Geoff had said that he would like us to leave him an hour free in the morning, to let him wake an hour earlier than us. He wanted time on his own to have a cup of tea and write his diary, but for some reason, this had not registered with me. Ronny and I wrote our diaries in the evening when Geoff was cooking. As a result, Geoff used to rise at 4 o'clock and I would rise only fifteen minutes later, depriving him of forty-five minutes of peace and solitude. I could, of course, have stayed in bed another hour, though that depended on whether or not the wind was blowing. If the wind was blowing, I could never stay in bed. If it was calm, it would have been wonderful to have an extra hour in bed. I was only keen on getting up if I was looking forward to the day, and clearly, a windless day was not one to look forward to.

It was not until we discussed the issues at the end of the whole journey that I discovered that he found me getting up so soon after him had put him under pressure to push on. This was not my intention. Had it registered with me, that he wanted an hour on his own in the early morning, I would have given it to him.

As long as we were not going to run late.

On that day, December 18, we still had 13 ½ miles to reach the Thiel Mountain cache, not just to exchange our sledges, but also to dump cooking fuel that we felt was surplus to our needs. To get there, we were required to deviate off the direct course we were taking to Hercules Inlet, and head west. There were snowstorms during the night, and we had to mend our sledges, but that was time not really wasted because the weather was poor. But we never really got started. There was no wind to speak off, and after having done only 0.3 miles, we made camp again. It was a double bad day because not only did we have to divert to the west, but also we had hoped to get past our halfway point. Making a diversion just to dump some excess fuel felt like a waste of time, but the excess fuel was extra weight, and for environmental and conservation reasons we could not just dump it on the ice.

Geoff was regretting not taking more photographs. I was surprised he did not have the right type of camera for snapshots. He took a big Nikon camera, unlike Ronny and I who had small cameras in our top pockets, so we were easily able to use them, whipping them out of our pockets and snapping away. Geoff carried his big camera in his sledge. In the same way that I only used my video camera two or three times, he only used his camera two or three times. It was a hassle getting it out and preparing it. My camera was a small modern digital, where his was an old-fashioned film camera.

## FRIDAY, DECEMBER 19, 2003

A big day, despite starting slowly. There was little wind, and I was bursting with frustration, at the same time careful not to show it (as much as I could). If we had not been trying to tack to the fuel cache, I grumbled privately to myself, we would not be so delayed. Going straight for Hercules Inlet with our kites, we could have made better progress.

On the other hand, Thiel fuel cache was where we had agreed to swap our sledges, even though we knew they would not come that day. We still had more fuel than we felt we needed, and at the fuel cache we were going to drop off 15 litres of white spirit. It was an extra load, and ran the risk of bursting in the sledge, and we always wanted to reduce weight in our sledges. If we left the white spirit at the fuel cache, then it would be there for another expedition to use; the only other fuel at the cache was for the aircraft. Either way, the aircraft would leave our spare fuel there, or fly it back to Patriot Hills. There would not be any sledges there, so without the fuel drop we really could have continued to head directly north.

We had already had a fuel leak in the gallons of white spirit, bubble-wrapped in a cardboard box, carried on my sledge. After a tough day and a lot of sledge battering, the fuel container broke and leaked. If we had not protected our food bags, the food could have been contaminated. Fortunately, none of our food was touched, only some of my clothing, which dried out.

Though the food bags were protected, some bags took a lot of damage from the constant banging of the sledge. The chocolate was a mass of small pieces when we opened it up.

Then the wind picked up!

There were two periods without wind, when we stood around our sledges, just waiting without making camp, always alert to the danger of getting too cold standing around. We were grateful when the wind came and then I got a good drive on.

In the lead, I just kept going.

The *sastrugi* was big. I had to focus on where I was skiing, and speeding along I did not find time to look behind because the conditions absorbed me. I had got past the mountains when I looked around and in the distance I saw Ronny, but no Geoff. I stopped and waited; it seemed like forever, before Ronny turned up. Still no Geoff. It was quite a long time before he appeared, the longest time that we had had to wait for someone out of sight to catch up on our journey.

There I was, having asked Geoff only two days earlier to ensure we stayed in closer contact, and I had caused the biggest split of the trip.

When Geoff turned up fifteen minutes later, it was a relief when I could see him. He appeared first as a kite out of the snow, getting taller and taller. He had been delayed because of conditions underfoot, and his sledge had rolled over a few times. The surface was not good, and he had been unlucky as we all were on various days. I had not seen it or sensed it and I had just kept going.

Geoff was cross. He said something that I did not completely hear. But I did feel guilty, and I did stay closer with him after that.

We were delayed finding the fuel cache. Geoff had it positioned on his GPS, where it had been in previous years, but it had been moved about a mile away. We finally found it because Ronny had taken a GPS position for the cache on the flight into the South Pole. Having found the new cache and dropped the fuel we did not need, we carried on in excellent conditions and had a wonderful journey. In my notebook I wrote, "surface the best we have seen, in the next 5 hours we gain another 27 miles, our second-best day." The total distance that day was 40.7 miles, of which 35 were made using kites in a day lasting 11 hours. We had climbed back above 5,000 feet, at 5,540 feet, with 270 miles to go.

But Geoff's sledge was starting to break up. Ronny's sledge was bad, and so was mine, now Geoff's started to disintegrate. We relied on knowing we had back-up and raced past the halfway point in those conditions, remaining up-beat, despite being past where Mike had agreed to drop the sledges off.

As a result of our daily call to base camp, we knew we were going to have to go a couple of days without the new sledges, not just because of the weather, but because there had been an emergency at Patriot Hills. Colin Bodill and Jennifer Murray had crashed their helicopter in a whiteout 100 miles north of the base, that is, even further away from us, and been seriously injured. All Mike Sharp's aircraft resources were used on that rescue. Mike would have done a normal fuel run into Thiel that day, but obviously this was not a priority with two lives at stake. We were going to get resupplied when there were no other priorities at base camp. That suited me. It meant we could keep going, knowing that when we wanted the resupply, we could have it. Because the surface had changed, we were now making brilliant progress. The wind was much the same, but it was the better surface that made it so much easier.

## SATURDAY, DECEMBER 20, 2003

On this day we made the best mileage so far, but I still felt disappointed. There had been two previous days when there were differences of opinion about whether we should be using different sizes of sail, 5 or 10 metres. Now conditions had improved I wanted to use the faster sail, the 10 metre instead of the 5 metre, as much as possible. We all had to use the same size sail, or the expedition split up. We had tried once to allow one person to ski with one size sail, and another with a different size, at their choice, and it did not work. It was a question of how much risk we were prepared to take, balanced against the speed we were prepared to travel.

At least, that was how I saw it.

There was an argument that the faster we went, if conditions were not quite right, the bigger potential we had for injury, and speed also caused sledges to roll more frequently. More haste, in other words, less speed. As Geoff's sledge lost more and more of its integrity, so his views about risk became more cautious. I spent much of the day worrying that I had asked Mike Sharp for only two new sledges instead of three, but I felt sure Mike would deliver three as there were three sledges in the ice cave (he confirmed this later that day).

But the doubts I had about using under-sized sails, on Geoff's call, had to be handled carefully. The harmony of the group was critical to an enjoyable expedition. While any issues needed to be confronted immediately – if they were not, they became worse – I had to be sensitive. I had asked Geoff to join the trip because he was an experienced Antarctic traveller. How could I, with nothing like his experience, challenge his view of the size of the sail we were using? Yet I felt I could live with a faster sail, and Ronny certainly could. Ronny sat between us in the tent in the evening while we were discussing these things, but said nothing. Ronny knew he was an invited guest on this trip. He would have his views, but would not dream of undermining either one of us, and did not want to voice his opinions.

That evening Geoff told me about the injury problems to his arm, which forced him to err on the side of caution in picking the sail he wanted to travel with.

Though we had more problems with the sledges, I still dreamt I could get through with my original coat of arms, almost a fetish now with me. We were running out of rope to tie the sledges together, and discussed whether we could put one sledge inside a second one. What made me optimistic was Geoff's confidence that he would get us through, and bring the old sledges home. I believed he was capable of that. I was not quite sure how he would have achieved it, but he was confident it was possible. That gave me confidence, even though the sledges were in danger of splitting in half; they were just held together by rope. There was not much of the sledges left to be held together.

Despite our problems, we covered 47 miles, an amazing distance considering how many times my sledge rolled over.

## SUNDAY, DECEMBER 21, 2003

It was a sunny day, with a temperature of minus 14. We spent 2-½ hours mending sledges before we set out. Ronny's was the worst. We got 8 hours' travelling in, including a lunch break.

The good surface disappeared and rough *sastrugi* returned. It became difficult again, adding to the damage on the sledges. I had a really bad day with my sledge rolling over. I was as angry about the conditions as I had been on the whole trip. Because I was not near any of my companions during this period, I could do all the shouting I wanted. I was so angry.

Why was it my sledge that kept rolling over?

It turned over, I righted it, travelled five minutes and it turned over again.

Each time I had to take off my skis, bring down the kite, struggle with the wind blowing the kite off course, untangle the lines, get the sledge upright, skis on again, pull the kite back in the air, 200 yards and the sledge rolled over again!

It was not happening to anyone else. Why was it not happening to anyone else? Of course I took it personally. I blamed my technique, but then on other days it happened to Geoff or Ronny, who had no problems with their technique. We could not explain why it was that on any one day, one of us suffered from turnovers more than the others. Sometimes it even happened on a piece of flat ice.

It was a bad day, made worse after lunch because Ronny was keen to meet up with an expedition coming the other way, from Patriot Hills to the Pole.

Almost all the expeditions to the South Pole telephoned in their co-ordinates every night to Patriot Hills. These included Pen Hadow and Simon Murray, and a Korean expedition. We monitored their progress and noted that we were likely to come across one expedition led by the American woman guide, Matty McNair. One of the four expeditioners was Alex Blyth, who worked in the City of London for the *Financial News*. They were making the best progress of all the expeditions to the South Pole, and we were likely to come across them first.

There were also two women – Rosie Stancer and Fiona Thornhill – racing to the Pole but trying to pretend it was not a race, though each wanted to be the first woman solo to make that journey. They did not give Patriot Hills their co-ordinates, because each did not want the other to know her position, so this information was also not available to us.

With Ronny's urging, we knew we could travel 20 miles just slightly out of our longitude and meet Matty McNair's expedition. It was out of our way because we were not on the right longitude for them, but Ronny took it upon himself to head further east than we needed to. That meant attacking the *sastrugi* at almost a 90-degree angle. It was really hard skiing and unnecessarily damaging to our sledges, I felt, just to find these walkers.

On expeditions, one big attraction was the feeling I got when I achieved something difficult, but this did not include the thought of meeting others in the middle of nowhere. I thought the McNair expedition would be asleep when we found them, because we were skiing at night with the sun behind us, and coming the other way they would have wanted the sun behind them too. They would move when we slept, and vice versa. But we kept going further and further east and we could not see the tents. The longer this went on, the more I grumbled to myself about why we were heading this far east.

In the end, I got annoyed.

I felt that Ronny was thinking more about meeting up with this other expedition than with us achieving our goal. It turned out that the co-ordinates that we had for the others were from the day before. We did find, through the GPS, their campsite, which they had left perfectly clean. We found where they had used the snow for building up their tents, and their footprints, which was awesome enough, footprints in the middle of nowhere. But we had made that diversion for nothing.

I told Ronny shortly that I felt it was an unnecessary escapade.

This was the only time I commented on Ronny's participation. He was a fantastic member of the team. If they ever commented on my behaviour, either I did not listen or I cannot remember. I had a different relationship with each of my companions.

With Ronny, when I had asked him to get himself down to South America and from then on, he was my guest, I paid all his expenses, I did not pay him a wage, even though he was as helpful as Geoff in making the trip successful. It was a professional job for Geoff, and the deal included wages, all part of the package.

For Ronny, we were on a journey he really wanted to do, and I had given him a unique opportunity at little financial cost to himself. Ronny was grateful for this chance. What he brought to the adventure was his experience of both sailing and kiting, as well as previous time on expeditions, though normally of just one or two weeks long. He took it as a great compliment to be asked to join the trip, and although he had a lot of experience, he chose to play a supportive role and never swanked about it. There were parts of the trip where I suggested that he led, in repairing equipment, for example, and he was immensely valuable and wanted to show it.

His big concern throughout was any chance of failure in the areas where he had made decisions, in choosing the correct sails and kites. He had consulted with the best sail maker in Germany, Wolf Beringer, and with the highly experienced Polar traveller, Borge Ousland, who had crossed both the Arctic and the Antarctic. Ronny took professional advice on what sails we should take, but in the end he had individual responsibility and wanted to make sure his selection had been correct.

With Ronny I felt that I understood the relationship.

With Geoff, I did not always know what he was thinking at certain times of the trip. He might have felt that because he was being paid, it was not his place to voice his opinion. I came to feel at times that there was a crucial difference in the relationship between Ronny and me, and between Geoff and me.

Was it the fact that money had changed hands with one and not the other?

I know that Geoff would not have been there had I not paid him. If it was a trip that Geoff had really wanted to go on, a journey completely new to him, then perhaps he would have done it for nothing or for the new experience. As it was something he had done before, if he was going to do it again, naturally he wanted to be paid for it. The irony was that Antarctic expeditions involving ski sails and kites probably number less than four.

There was no actual fact that I could pick on, but I remained unsure about the real difference in my relationships with the two men. Geoff did not get angry easily, or open up to his true thoughts. I have the utmost respect for him as a professional and a companion to travel with on an expedition. However, I do not know to this day what Geoff thought of me or the way I handled myself.

We complied with the 5 o'clock rule that day, having covered another good distance, 32 miles. In discussion that evening, we thought the *sastrugi* seemed never-ending, but we were down to half the height of the South Pole, 4,798 feet with 190 miles to go.

## MONDAY, DECEMBER 22, 2003

We finished breakfast and made our call to Base Camp to inform them where we were and when we were leaving. They told us that the Twin Otter aircraft was already in the air, delivering fuel to the Thiel cache, and would drop by us on its return journey to deliver replacement sledges. We felt that the pilot would be the best judge of a place to land, and made ready with our sledges packed and our kites out so that wherever he did land, we would ski to him. We assumed he would land to the north of us, so we would not go back on ourselves. Geoff thought it probable he would not be able to land exactly where we were, which is why we were prepared to move.

In the event the pilot landed just to the north of our campsite and taxied up to us. Geoff said his name was Karl, with the reputation of being one of the best pilots in the world in a Twin Otter. Landing where he did proved Geoff's belief in him.

By now two of our original sledges were in such poor condition that they were later scrapped in the rubbish heap in Chile. They could never be used again (I brought mine, still with my coat of arms, all the way home). They could have continued to be used if the surface was fair, but one bad day of *sastrugi* would have wiped them out. If we could have guaranteed smoother ice, then maybe we could have got them through.

The aircraft took our old sledges back to Base Camp, and we set off with our new – fibreglass – sledges. They were the same design as the Kevlar sledges, and like them they rolled over. The irony was, I did not have a bad time with the new sledge and found mine a big improvement, but Geoff now had problems. His sledge kept rolling over, and we could not find a logical reason why.

Despite this, we did a good mileage. The new sledges were heavier than our previous sledges, and therefore had more structural integrity. Sometimes, when righting the sledges after they had gone over, it was only necessary to grab one end to twist it upright. When the structural integrity went on the Kevlar sledges we needed to use two hands, cradling it like a baby, to roll it upright.

I was conscious of not being too far apart from my companions towards the end of the day, Geoff in particular because he had the tent. One day I was some distance behind and we were becalmed. If we were becalmed for any length of time we had to make camp, just to protect ourselves against the cold. If Geoff stopped for the day because the wind had dropped to nothing, then I faced a long, difficult man-hauling journey to catch up with him without the assistance of the wind. On this occasion we did not actually make camp, but it took me a long time walking without wind-assistance to catch up and for the three of us to meet. At the time it was easier for us to move towards where Ronny was, because he was further east than either of us. Ronny was even further away from me than Geoff, so I had the longest journey to make without wind.

From that point on, when the conditions were light, I made sure I was either out in front and they had to come to me, or I would be very close to Geoff, even if he was not exactly following the path I wanted him to go.

There were times when I thought I could see much better ways of going forward than Geoff or Ronny. When driving a car, no one looks at the road immediately in front of the car. You look as far forward as you can see. It was the same when skiing with the sail in front. I looked at the *sastrugi* right in front of me to avoid the worst bits by going around them, but I also looked ahead to create the path to reduce the *sastrugi* as much as possible.

Even if I saw a better way through I stayed close to Geoff in case the wind dropped, because I did not want a long windless trek to catch him.

I became aware that there was more wear and tear on my body. In the last seven days, after skiing for 5 hours or more, my knees had begun to hurt. I skied for the last four hours of every day with my knees in pain. This did not stop me skiing, because I had to get the job done. I had never believed that I would go on a trip like this and not get some pain. It was modest pain compared to what I had thought I might have to put up with. All I hoped was that I had not done any permanent damage to them.

We had made good progress during the day, despite winds as low as 6 to 10 knots. After 7-½ hours skiing with many short stops but no lunch, we had done 40.4 miles. We camped well below 5,000 feet, at 4,311 feet, having covered 436 miles, with 150 to go.

That evening I made Christmas telephone calls by satellite. I rang work, where I knew they would be starting to break up for their holidays. This was really a Christmas signing off with them. I was behaving as normally as possible, I think, by making those phone calls. I only rang work that day, the last day before Christmas.

I always kept the battery for my satellite phone in my chest pocket. This was insurance. On previous cold-weather trips I had kept a satellite phone battery in my left-hand breast pocket, to keep it warm. There was not a real necessity to do that because we had a solar panel to recharge the phones, which it could do in three or four hours. Yet I persisted in my private insurance game, keeping the spare battery close to my chest 24 hours a day. It never left my clothing. I could take it straight out of my pocket, put it into the phone, and communicate again. Despite a solar panel, I did not change my cautious habits.

We went to sleep listening to the wind getting stronger.

## TUESDAY, DECEMBER 23, 2003

We started the day with a strong ambition to travel a "one degree day", that is 60 miles. On previous days we felt we could have achieved this goal had things been slightly different. We set out believing it was a possibility and within the first couple of minutes Geoff and I had collided with each other.

In an attempt to avoid him, I dropped my sail on to the back of his sledge!

We had started off at the same time, too close together, and should have allowed more distance between us. If it had been a car accident, it would have been a 50/50 knock for knock. He may have overtaken me too closely, but when he came past, I pulled aside and he obviously got a better wind-tow than I had, because suddenly I could not go straight ahead because of the *sastrugi*. I wanted to go to the right to avoid it, but when I turned to the right he was in my way. A good wind was blowing and I tried to avoid him by dropping my sail, but it hit the back of his sledge and damaged 6 or 7 lines.

What had started as a promising day had a 45-minute period lopped off the front of it, in cold conditions, repairing the sail. It was the worst sail accident of the whole trip. Tension remained quite high during the five hours ski sailing that followed because Geoff insisted on using the 10 SqM sail, when a 14 SqM would have enabled us to go faster. Then at around midnight, the weather closed in. The contrast was bad, visibility was poor, and we could not see the horizon or even judge the condition of the *sastrugi*. Conditions turned into a whiteout, where we could not see 20 yards, and barely see each other.

At 1215 I said we should call it a day.

Our tempers were not improved by what happened as we unpacked to make camp. Normally, when breaking camp every morning, we all had different duties. Ronny played his part in tidying up the external part of the tent. Geoff carried the sledge and most of the cooking equipment, while I carried food and fuel. Geoff tidied up inside the tent, and was last to leave it, which left us to break down the tent. Ronny would often be the person who rolled up the flysheet. As soon as Geoff was out of the tent, down it came and Ronny prepared it and left it next to Geoff's sledge, not in a bag, just wrapped up.

That morning Geoff had felt the wrapping of the tent was not good enough to go on his sledge, and threw the tent quite violently on the ground, saying it was not done properly. He then refolded the tent himself. I can remember that when he threw it on the ground, a number of tent poles went flying some distance. I picked up the furthest pole and put it back, and offered to help re-packing, but Geoff did not need any help.

When we unravelled the tent at the end of the day, there was a pole missing.

At first, no one said anything, but something had to be said, so I said it.

"I'm pleased you left it behind, Geoff, and not me."

Ronny did not say anything. We had the remainder of the tent poles, but it meant the tent sagged a bit, ironically over Geoff's side of the tent. Geoff did not say anything either. The following day Geoff packed up the tent himself and put it on his sledge. Ronny never packed the tent again. We never lost any more poles. Ronny did the flysheet but nothing more.

We had dropped to a height of 4,269 feet above sea level, and travelled 19.8 miles, a cumulative total of 457 miles. There were only 130 miles to go.

## DECEMBER 24, 2003.

There was a reasonably good following wind when we woke, but not good enough to use sails, so we used kites. It was how I felt the second leg should be, leaving the plateau and starting a serious descent; ice conditions in particular were so much better. But Geoff had a particularly bad day with his sledge rolling over, and he got angry with himself, as earlier on the journey I had got angry with myself, because he could not understand why his sledge was rolling over. There were lots of delays.

Until we were close to the end of our journey, when the sledges rolled over they normally rolled on to their side. Then they became a drag, so I knew what had happened. I had to stop, look around and see it was pulling against the harness because it was no longer on its runners. I stopped and suffered no injury at all. But towards the end of the journey, on two occasions the sledge rolled 360 degrees, landing back on its runners. This made the Pulk arms cross over. Then when I stopped it took me straight off my feet. After such a roll, unless I looked back to check, because the sledge was back on its runners there was no resistance, so when I stopped it bowled me over. The second time it bent me double, which was dangerous. I could have been seriously hurt, either by breaking my leg or injuring my back.

With all the confidence that I had built up about ski sailing, I had not focussed on this happening. Had it happened at the beginning of the journey, I would have carried the fear of it with me every day. I was grateful it occurred towards the end of the trip.

On paper this could have been a one-degree day, if we had not had so many stoppages. Geoff was particularly concerned with safety that day, and we reduced the lines on our kites from 50 metres to 30 metres. When we found that 30 metres was not fast enough, we went back to 50; each change took half an hour. If we had not made those changes we could have got a lot more miles done.

Meanwhile, despite all that dentist's attention in Santiago, I had a broken tooth. It came from eating nuts. I sat down that evening and wrote a summary, with Christmas approaching and after nearly four weeks travelling, of my ailments.

The first casualties were my knees, closely followed by my still-running nose, and then my shoulders and teeth. My feet could have been better, but were holding up. The most difficult thing to live with was having an itchy dry scalp. I always wore a hat, night and day, slept in a hat and skied with a hat, and I had never imagined I would have problems with my scalp. It was because I was not washing my hair. After years of a daily hair wash, not washing it for more than three weeks was uncomfortable.

I found that I had written in the wrong co-ordinates for Hercules Inlet, which meant I had to adjust my mind for another 20 miles, but I felt so on top of what was happening that this was not a big problem. We had had some big days and knew we only had 110 odd miles to go. We could complete in just two good day's travelling, and we still had food for another 10 days. The journey was cracked, and if it was not done and dusted, we were nearly there. Paradoxically, I definitely did not want it to be over until it was absolutely over, and not one minute less. I wanted it to be completely successful.

It could yet fail, if the Antarctic turned on us with even 130 miles to go, or I picked up an injury.

I did think about injuries constantly, and what I would do if one of us – not me – were incapacitated. It would be a decision for all three of us. If I were left on the ice with either Ronny or Geoff, would I have gone on? Yes, definitely. We never discussed this, but in my own head I allowed it to happen. As long as we got the third person to safety, I would not have stopped.

As for losing both companions through injury, it would have depended how close to the end of the journey I was. It was hardly likely to happen. One person picking up an injury was a definite possibility. Two people? God, we would have had to be an unlucky expedition for that to happen. An injury, I thought, was not going to happen, because I was very upbeat about the success of the mission.

This was a 40 miles day, and we dropped 1,000 feet.


## THURSDAY, DECEMBER 25, 2003 – CHRISTMAS DAY.

We woke at the normal time of 4 o'clock in the afternoon, and found a complete whiteout and little wind!

Snow was coming from the north, the direction we wanted to travel. We rang Patriot Hills to find out what their weather was like, as we felt we were in their weather system. They told us they expected it to be bad for a couple of days. I feared we were going to spend Christmas Day and Boxing Day sitting in the tent. On the two important days of the year we were going to be sitting there, not moving!

It was the complete negation of a dream I had had eighteen months earlier.

Boxing Day, December 26, 2003, was my 50th birthday, an important date in a man's life, especially one who aspired, as I did, to physical adventure. In the summer of 2002, I had a vision of how I would spend my 50th birthday, doing the best ski sailing of my life in Antarctica. I did not have to cudgel my brain to get this vision; having seen conditions there in 1995, it took very little imagination to conjure up how bright the sunshine would be, and how brilliant the weather was when it behaved itself. This vision saw me through the last eighteen months of my preparations, and encouraged me through every setback.

So when the real Christmas Day came and we looked out of the tent at a whiteout, I was as sick as a pig.

Clearly the weather was so bad that it was not just Christmas Day that could be ruined, but Boxing Day as well. Were we destined to stagnate there for two days, as Patriot Hills forecast?

I felt emotional.

I had spoken to my two daughters, Isabel and Marina, on Christmas Eve. This had made me guilty that they were in England and I was thousands of miles away from them, halfway across Antarctica. It was nothing they said, it was just talking to them that made me feel guilty, that I was not there with them. Throughout the journey, I had focussed on completing it. The idea of sitting in a tent with two other men in the middle of nowhere, not moving, when I could have been at home with my family, was no good at all.

I started to feel hacked off. I had always believed that, one way or another, I had made sound judgements. Now I began to question whether I was right.

Part of it was feeling sick at the thought that my dream was not coming true.

*No wind at journey's end, reduced to walking.* © Ronny Finsaas

*Ronny removing his Ski Skins at Hercules Inlet.*

*Arrival at Hercules Inlet, with thanks to one of our charity supporters.*

*Twin Otter arrives 8 hours after base camp learns we have arrived at Hercules Inlet.*

*Patriot Hills on our return, with many more tents and civilised facilities.*

*The DC-3 stuck in ice, under repair (it's now back in service).*

*Blue Ice runway at Patriot Hills.*

*Hot bath a prospect as we load aircraft to return to Punta Arenas.*

Looking out of the tent, discussing what Patriot Hills had said, the consensus was that it would be at least a day before the weather improved.

We sat for 11 hours, just watching the weather.

I opened one birthday card from my sister Jayne during this barren period.

At 3 o'clock in the morning, normally two hours from the end of a full day's travelling, we thought the weather had improved. Driven men, we tore into breaking camp and packed our sledges, anything to travel, even if it was just 10 miles, perhaps just for 2 hours. I wanted to do something, anything, by way of celebration that I was approaching the big five-O.

Technically, at 3 o'clock in the morning local time, it was certainly my birthday back in England, so I felt we were setting off as a birthday treat.

By a miracle, the weather improved enough that we threw out the 5 o'clock rule and kept on travelling until 7.30 in the morning, extending our day 2-½ hours. After that time the sun was virtually in front of us and hitting us in the eyes, and even had we wanted to it would not have been appropriate to keep going.

In those 4 hours of driven ski sailing, we covered 20 miles. This was a real bonus. We made camp and went to bed about 10 o'clock in the morning.

## FRIDAY, DECEMBER 26, 2003 – BOXING DAY

In our inverted day, even though we woke every afternoon, we acted as if it was a morning, the real beginning of the day. In fact, we did 20 miles on the morning of Boxing Day, my birthday, had 6 hours sleep, and when we woke we treated the day as if it was the beginning of our real Boxing Day trip.

Now another miracle happened.

On the real Boxing Day, we woke at 4pm, looked out of the tent and discovered that conditions were good. We could not believe the change from the previous day; so much for weather forecasts in the Antarctic. We started skiing with the kite at 7 o'clock in the evening, and the surface was the best that we had experienced.

In the first 4 hours we did 25 miles, this with our kites!

The wind improved and we switched to sails and did another 26 miles, our biggest distance of the whole trip. In fact, we used every size of sail we had with us, and on my real 50th birthday we did 51 miles.

It was exactly how I had imagined it was going to be in my original dream.

I knew from my diary I had lots of bad falls, but I do not remember them. The real Boxing Day was a double win. The previous day I had been thinking that we still needed three good days of skiing to get to Hercules Inlet, and that we were destined for two days of not skiing, which would have left us with 6 days left to do the journey. Suddenly, we had 20 miles under our belt, and now another 51, a total of 71, to break the back of the whole trek.

Only something stupid could stop us completing in the time available.

We made camp, jubilantly. Geoff went in as normal, and as normal I was the last one into the tent. But when I got in I saw that Geoff had put up birthday bunting he had been given by my wife, Christina. He had also put up balloons (I had not heard him blowing them up) while I was outside. Geoff handed me birthday cards from my children, from Christina and my parents.

I felt tears come to my eyes. I did not want to show how emotionally affected I was by the gesture, but it made me feel good.

Then Ronny disappeared out of the tent. When he returned he gave me a square box of ice with a ribbon around it. I opened it and there I found he had bought a South Pole Leatherman! This was an extraordinary present.

(When we were at the South Pole, invited in by the Americans to get our passports stamped, we noticed a small gift shop there for American workers. Ronny had bought himself a Leatherman tool, which he had used several times on our trip. It was a "South Pole Leatherman", and when I saw Ronny use it I had thought, "I really wished I'd seen one of those, I'd have bought one"; they cannot be bought elsewhere in the world. I felt I had missed out by not buying one, but Ronny did not know that I thought that. When he gave me one as a birthday present, I was overwhelmed. The penknife was more than I wanted. It was very moving, especially as he had bought it before he knew how the trip was going to go.)

A birthday I will never forget.


## DECEMBER 27, 2003

One good day would now see us reach Hercules Inlet. Facing a journey of just over 40miles, it was odd that for the first time I felt very tired. We got up at 6.20 in the evening. Obviously the previous day had been a big one, and we had not had a lot of sleep between Christmas and Boxing Day. I had thought at the beginning of the trip, with the amount of food we were eating that I was putting on weight (it *felt* like I was putting on weight) but it was now obvious that I was losing weight. I had shed 15 pounds, even though I had gone into the trip reasonably fit.

There was little wind and we started off using kites. Before we got halfway there, having covered a mere 18miles, I was struggling to keep up. If Geoff and Ronny had said, let's stop, for the first time I would have said, OK, let's stop. I had never felt like that before. I did not know whether it was because the journey was almost done, but I did feel that last day made us work hard at it.

We had to go up an incline with little wind and everything in my body aching, especially my shoulders. I could see in the distance, quite big nanutaks (small hills of rock), but I could only see the peaks of them. As I could only see the small peak, I thought that if I could get that much further there would be a slight decline and then the wind would pick up. I prayed for the wind to pick up to get me through the struggle of the last 20 miles.

It was not my call to stop and break the journey into two days. The other two were well out in front of me, and there was no way of communicating with them. I could not stop because they were so far in front, even though I was really struggling. My technique on the kite was exposed with so little wind. Going up that last hill, I suffered. But when we broke over the top, just that little extra wind enabled me to overcome my technique failures and I was able to catch up and move on.

In a short distance we dropped 2,000 feet, choosing to use the smallest sail, 5 SqM, because the wind had picked up sharply. We could not travel too fast because of the steepness of the slope, with the wind driving off the mountains straight into the inlet and the sea. I had a bad time with my sledge, with nine overturns in half an hour. Then the ice levelled out and we really started to move. The sun was out, it was warm – only minus 7 degrees – and wonderful, and we started a conversation about where the end of the journey was, exactly.

Suddenly, the wind stopped blowing. Absolutely nothing.

It was a flat calm. Where had the wind gone?

I turned to ask Geoff: "How much further have we got to go?"

He said: "We're here."

I said: "We can't be here, because we're still going somewhere."

He said: "Look around you, this is Hercules Inlet."

I said: "I'm sorry, it isn't Hercules Inlet."

He said: "You've seen the map as well as I have."

I said: "Yes, I have seen the map."

But I was not happy.

I had asked Geoff at the beginning of the journey where would it end, and was told, you don't need to know that yet but it is at 80/80 (that is, south 80 degrees, west 80 degrees). We had put in the co-ordinates for the crevasses and the different waypoints, and the only place I did not have on my GPS was where we were going to finish.

I came to the snap conclusion that the original "80/80" answer was too glib.

I had pored over the map every night for the past four weeks, and seen that 80/80 was not exactly Hercules Inlet. We may have been 80 degrees West, but we needed to be further north to be in Hercules Inlet. Even if we were already slightly further north than 80 degrees, the chances were that we were still not actually in Hercules Inlet.

"How high should we be at the Inlet?" I asked Geoff.

He said: "About a thousand feet."

And indeed, we were 1,050 feet up. But of course, the point was that I was not mentally prepared for the trip to finish. We had been going along and suddenly we stopped, but this was only because the wind stopped. When I was told that the trip was over, I was not prepared to accept this was true just because the wind had stopped blowing.

"I'm sorry," I said, "we're not there".

Geoff said: "Well, where do you want to go?"

"I'll tell you where I want to go," I said, "when I get there."

I was not prepared to discuss it. I took off my skis, put on my walking boots, packed the kite and sails and skis on to the sledge and set off. Walking.

The other two followed me.

"We're going to carry on," I called over my shoulder.

They agreed to carry on and follow me (at least, they followed me). We walked for an hour and ten minutes. I watched the GPS all the time. Then we got to 80 degrees West by my GPS.

"Now we're finished", I said.

We were 79.56 degrees south, and 80 degrees west. That was right for Hercules Inlet. Where we had originally stopped was not.

And, of course, the end of the journey was not going to be decided by the wind.

The end of the journey was when I said it was going to be.

It had, after all, been my dream.

We made camp there, with 800 feet of ice between sea level and us. It was sea ice, as opposed to land ice, that was the difference. The object of the whole journey was to ski from the South Pole to the sea. We came off the mountains and we were now definitely on the flat seawater ice.

We phoned Patriot Hills. They said they would pick us up, as the contract stipulated, as soon as they could. It was a taxi service, not a rescue. They picked us up eight hours later. We were taken back to Patriot Hills, and though it was our morning, they offered us Sunday roast beef and roast potatoes and beer. We ate hungrily.

Ronny stayed on with the Malaysian girl to teach her how to ski sail over the following two weeks, and was given a tent of his own. Geoff kept the one we had been using. I went into the torn one that had been left behind. There was plenty of room for one.

I felt a great sense of relief at what had been achieved. Until it was done, I always felt something could take it away from me. It was the end of eight year's dreaming and two and a half years planning. Every time there had been problems, I had overcome them. Down to the last 40 miles, my head said the trip was done but I could not accept this until we reached the sea ice.

I had been to the South Pole in 1995 as a passenger and a tourist. I was not intentionally in that position, but that was what I felt when Robert Swan had not come with me. Many people take the opportunity to visit the Pole for the experience of having done so. The professionals, the Polar peer group, obviously treat them civilly.

But they are not part of the Polar scene, and back then, I was very conscious of that.

After arriving back at Patriot Hills that day I felt I had crossed over the long difficult bridge from being a passenger to being included.

*I now need something else!*

# Antarctica Diary, 2003/4

**Nov 26, Wednesday**  Left Heathrow 11.30pm (2 hours late). No excess charge + upgrade to 1st class.

**Nov 27, Thursday**  Arrived San Paulo, 8.45am local. 1030 flight to Santiago left at 1130. Arrived Santiago 1430. Glued teeth. Left Santiago 1900, arrived Punta Arenas 2330. Journey: 28.5 hours.

**Nov 28, Friday**  Up at 0630 ready for 0700 flight to Antarctica – too windy. Updates 0900, 1100, 1400, 1900. 2100, no go.

**Nov 29, Saturday**  0700, 0900, fixed back, 1100, 1400, 1700, 1900 reports on conditions. Still no go.

**Nov 30, Sunday**  Depart Punta Arenas, 2230 local, arrive Patriot Hills 0300 Chilean (and local) time on Dec 1 . Unload 0530, put up tent, sleep at 0800 for 2 ½ to 3 hours.

**Dec 1, Monday**  Strong winds all night and day, up to 60 mph. Need a windless half-day to fly to Pole.

**Dec 2, Tuesday**  Good night, wind reduced. Pen Hadow/Simon Murray left on foot for Pole. We expect to fly to the Pole at 10am tomorrow. Must rise 0600. Americans invite us to see the South Pole station.

**Dec 3, Wednesday**    Minus 38 degrees. Left Patriot Hills, 1005. Arrive Thiel Mountain 1233, left 1341, arrived South Pole 1556. Dinner, made camp. Started to suffer altitude sickness. Face journey 607 NMs, walking 698 statute miles, sick as a dog.

**Dec 4, Thursday**    Woke 0700, severe altitude headache, US doctor gave me 4 hours oxygen, 2 litres of saline drip. Felt better. Left at 1900 hrs (12.30 GMT), 10 minute stops every 2 hours, temperature – 39 degrees. Now on "Sun" hours (-0530 GMT). Travelled 16.2 NMs to S89.43.899, W86.10.647.

**Dec 5, Friday**    Left 1845, travelled 4 miles in 2 hours. Wind died, 1 mile in 2 hours, then 2 ½ hours for 4 miles, totalling 8.6nms. Camped 0???, S89.35.420, W 92.34.030. Tough day. Cumulative 24.6nms.

**Dec 6, Saturday**    Left 1830. Little wind, 100 yards in 2 ½ hours, camped, lunch, more wind, left at 2400, 20 nms in 5 ½ hours. Camped 0630, S89.15.650, W88.23.111. Very cold. Cumulative 44.6nms.

**Dec 7, Sunday**    Left 0745. Very tough time, fell continuously. Wind improved, then made progress. Travelled 29.2NMs, camped S 88.46.553, W 87.48.376, 9,057 feet. Cumulative 73.8nms

**Dec 8, Monday**    Windy night, but faded. Made 100 yards. Camped S88.46.327, W 89.52.008, 9,043 feet. Cumulative 73.9 nms.

**Dec 9, Tuesday**    Woke 1330, very windy since 1100. Left camp, 1810, skied 10 hours, only one rest. Travelled 36.9NMs in good wind, poor visibility. Camped 0420, S8808552, W9040.573, 8,887 feet. Cumulative 111 nms.

**Dec 10, Wednesday**    Weather closed in from north, little wind in wrong direction. Visibility poor. Did not move from tent. Travelled 0 NMs, still 111nms cumulative total.

**Dec 11, Thursday**    No movement, weather still from north. Need a great wind. Zero nms, S88.08.552, W 90.40.573, 8,886 feet still 111 cumulative nms.

**Dec 12, Friday**    Left early, 1745, good vis, wind 10-15 knots, NE. Make 45nms in 11 hours, back on correct longitude, but sledges breaking up. Camped S 87.25.079, W 86.36.710, down to 7,844 feet. Cumulative 156 nms.

**Dec 13, Saturday**    Three hours mending sledges. Left 2300. Surface improving, good visibility, 25 nms in 6 hours. Camped at 6,949 feet, S 86.59.686, W86.18.059. Cumulative 181.

**Dec 14, Sunday**    Good start, wind and visibility, but then tough. Made 28.4 nms. Camped S86.31.766, W 87.27.867, at 6,414 feet. Need new sledges. Fuel spilt from my sledge. Cumulative 209.

**Dec 15, Monday**    Little wind, travelled 4.7 nms. Camped S 86.27.066, W 87.22.785, at 6,352 feet. 73.9 NMs to go to Thiel Mountains, 2nd waypoint. Cumulative 214.

**Dec 16, Tuesday**    Little wind, good surface, 6 hours travelling for 29.3 nms. Camped S85.57.766, W86.41.410, at 5,843 feet. Cumulative 243.

**Dec 17, Wednesday**  Left 1900, little wind, poor surface, very tired. Travelled 33 nms. Camped S85.25.776, W 86.37.139, at 4,936 feet. Cumulative 276 nms.

**Dec 18, Thursday**  Winds good all night, but dropped. Travelled just 0.3nms. Two hours repairing sledges. Camped S85.25.480, W86.38.430, at 5,114 feet. Cumulative 276nms.

**Dec 19, Friday**  Difficult conditions, becalmed twice, travelled 40.7 nms in 11-hour day. All 3 sledges breaking up. Camped 84.44.806, W 87.01.309, at 5,540 feet. Cumulative total 317, 270 to do.

**Dec 20, Saturday**  Left 1930 after sledge repairs, stopped at 0430, Frustrating day. Travelled 47 nms. Camped S83.59.832, W 84.58.888, at 5,364 feet. Cumulative 364nms, 233 to go.

**Dec 21, Sunday**  2 ½ hours mending sledges, then 8 hours travel to 0500 for 32 nms. Camped S83.27.702, W 83.49.012, at 4,798 feet. Cumulative 396nms, 190 to go.

**Dec 22, Monday**  New sledges delivered. Left 2100, travelled until 0430, covering 40.4 nms. Camped S82.47.330, W83.41.070, at 4,311 feet. Cumulative 436 nms, 150 to go.

**Dec 23, Tuesday**  Good weather, but worsens, stop early at 1215, travelled 19.8 nms. Camped S82.28.349, W 82.58.321 at 4,269 feet. Cumulative 456, 130 to do.

**Dec 24, Wednesday**  Left 1900, finish at 0500, variable weather. Travelled 40 nms, camped S81.48.890, W 81.53.707, 3,223 feet. Destination change from Patriot Hills, 89.5 nms, to Hercules Inlet 111 nms. Cumulative 496.

**Dec 25, Thursday**
*(Christmas Day)*  Woke 1600, white-out. Stayed in tent till 0300. Visability improves, did 20nms by 0730. Camped, S 81.29.349, W 81.22.714, 3,317 feet. Cumulative 516nms. Patriot Hills 69.8, Hercules Inlet 90.8.

**Dec 26, Friday**
*(my 50th birthday)*  Woke 1600, 6 hours sleep. Great day, total of 51 nms. Camped S 80.38.613, W 81.08.819. 3,045 feet. Patriot Hills 18.9, Hercules Inlet 40.5. Cumulative 567.

**Dec 27, Saturday**  Left 1900, 15 nms in 3 hours. Winds changed, travelled 40 nms total, last 1H10M walking without kite or sail. Camped at 0620, S79.56.486, W 79.59.474, at 876 feet. All ice, over sea.

**Dec 28, Sunday**  Arrived by air at Patriot Hills. Roast beef and first beer for six weeks. Had a shower, cold in tent.

**Dec 29, Monday**  First full day at Patriot Hills. Great to relax and chat with others about the journey.

**Jan 1, 2004.**  Last food bag.

Left **Jan 8**  via Punta Arenas. England on **Jan 11**.

| Item | cals/110 gm | protein | carbo | fats | gms/day | cal/day | from | 3 pax gms per day | 3 pax gms 30 days |
|---|---|---|---|---|---|---|---|---|---|
| Muesli | 380 | 9.6 | 58.4 | 5.6 | 120 | 450 | PA | 360 | 10800 |
| Flapjack | 450 | 4.5 | 51.4 | 15.1 | 60 | 270 | PA | 180 | 5400 |
| Chocolate | 500 | 7.8 | 0 | 29.4 | 100 | 500 | PA | 300 | 9000 |
| Nuts | 4-600 | 16 | 0 | 63 | 60 | 350 | PA | 180 | 5400 |
| Dried fruit | 300 | 2.1 | 69.3 | 0.4 | 60 | 165 | PA | 180 | 5400 |
| Dried meal | 4-500 | 22 | 52 | 12 | 100 | 500 | UK | 300 | 9000 |
| Salami | 500 | 22 | 1.7 | 49 | 65 | 325 | UK | 195 | 5850 |
| Cheese | 412 | 25.5 | 0.1 | 34.4 | 50 | 206 | UK | 150 | 4500 |
| Butter | 737 | 0.5 | 0 | 81.7 | 50 | 366 | PA | 150 | 4500 |
| Potato | 300 | 1.6 | 13.4 | 1.3 | 40 | 120 | PA | 120 | 3600 |
| Pasta | 345 | 6.6 | 34.3 | 2 | 40 | 135 | PA | 120 | 3600 |
| Cuppa soup | 400 | 4.9 | 57.9 | 19.4 | 30 | 110 | PA | 90 | 2700 |
| Cookies | 360 | 4 | 69 | 8 | 74 | 260 | PA | 222 | 6660 |
| Sled Biscuits | 450 | | | | 100 | 450 | UK | 300 | 9000 |
| Choc Drink | 424 | 8 | 66.4 | 14 | 25 | 106 | PA | 75 | 2250 |
| Milk - dry | 506 | 25.7 | | 28 | 50 | 250 | PA | 150 | 4500 |
| Sugar | 400 | | 100 | | 25 | 100 | PA | 75 | 2250 |
| Fruit drink | 350 | | 9 | 0.1 | 50 | 175 | PA | 150 | 4500 |
| Coffee | | | | | 2 sachets | 0 | PA | 15 | 450 |
| Tea | | | | | 3 bags | 0 | PA | 15 | 450 |
| TOTALS | | | | | 1099 | 4838 | | 3327 | 99810 |
| Fuel | | | | | 1/3 litre p/p/p/d | | PA | 1 litre | 30 litres |

| | | |
|---|---|---|
| Weight of food and fuel | | TOTAL 120810gms |
| Weight of food and fuel per person | | 40370gms |

*Expedition food allocation/calorie intake.*

# Postscript

**Mike Sharp** had teamed up with four partners to make ANI work through the 2003/4 seasons, "not quite in the red", and planned to open an office in Salt Lake City ahead of a full season's work in 2004/5. His partners were David Rootes and Nick Lewis, both formerly with the British Antarctic Survey, and Mike and Peter McDowell from Quark, the Antarctic cruise company. They own ANI – subject to a few payments to the parent group, GEI – and use the ANI brand name only for South Pole flights. Sharp says: "I think all the owners support the science down there and are keen to help the research along, as well as show the continent to those who want to go and see it."

**Ronny Finsaas** stayed on for his two weeks, teaching the Malaysian girl, Sharifah Mazlina Syed Abdul Kadir to ski sail, which was a big story in her native country. The Malaysian Government was said to believe that if western people could ski sail across Antarctica, why not Malaysians? It offered no finance to help her, but it did support her, and she found herself attracting a number of sponsors. Described as "tough and ambitious and determined and very nice", Sharifah plans to make the same journey in 2004/5 as I made in 2003/4, with Ronny Finsaas as her sole companion. They will sleep in separate tents.

**Simon Murray**, 63, accompanied by veteran Polar traveller Pen Hadow, made it to the Pole on January 28, 2004, after a journey of 58 days, well inside their 65-day target. The 607 mile journey, completed by man-hauling sledges weighing 275 pounds without kites or sails, was completed without re-supply or airdrop, and left Simon the oldest man ever to have trekked to the South Pole. They each lost fourteen pounds in weight, and raised quarter of a million pounds towards rebuilding the Royal Geographical Society building in West London.

**Jennifer Murray** and her co-pilot **Colin Bodill** crashed their helicopter in a whiteout 110 miles north of Patriot Hills, while heading north to Ushuaia, intending to fly up the west coast of America to the North Pole. Jennifer Murray dislocated an elbow in the crash, while Colin was more seriously injured, but though initially in their shirt-sleeves in Polar temperatures, Colin erected a tent, rescued Jennifer from the wreckage, put her into a sleeping bag and got her into the tent, and had lit a stove before collapsing in agony. They were rescued within 5 hours and flown to Punta Arena, where it was discovered Colin's back was broken. He was lucky not to be paralysed. Both recovered, and Colin was awarded a bronze medal by the Royal Humane Society for saving Jennifer's life.

The **Dakota** was repaired successfully, with the work being finished on the last day of the season. The aircraft was slid on her old skis down to the ice runway and took off on wheels in perfect weather. It had been checked out by a safety expert from Transport Canada, so it was flown back to Canada, where it took four month's work taking the aircraft to bits and ensuring a "proper repair" to certify it to carry passengers again. It was sold to a Russian company which planned to operate on the South African side of the Antarctic, but ANI will be able to lease it back if necessary.

**Misha** failed to get elected to the Russian *Duma*.

**Geoff Somers** is now giving business presentations in "motivation", "leadership" and "risk assessment". He has guided a scientist for 10 weeks in Greenland

and has been on an Artic ship lecturing. Ironically, he is also preparing his numerous expedition diaries for a book.

**Fiona Thornhill**, 37, walked the 607 miles to the South Pole in 42 days. She was the first British woman to walk solo and unaided to the Pole, and beat the previous fastest time of 44 days for walking or skiing. Her rival, Rosie Stancer, 43 – though both women denied they were racing each other – was only a short time behind her but I believe her route meant she had travelled 30 miles further.

**Family** – The real effect at home I felt much later, when I was back home. Having left the Pole and set off for Hercules Inlet, I was unable to contact Christina, and those answering the satellite phone were always giving an excuse for her absence. In fact, she was in hospital, suffering from an illness that could have been attributed to stress. She had not told me before I left how poorly she felt, but once I had gone she had seen her doctor who had immediately sent her to hospital for tests. She was kept in overnight; it turned out not to be serious, but still worrying. It was when she picked me up at the airport, that she told me for the first time that she had been ill. She had not wanted to tell me before I left as she had thought it would have added to the stresses I was already feeling.

Isabel had a similar reaction. She was at Bath University, and two days before I left for the Antarctic, I had driven down to say goodbye to her just before an exam, clearly unsettling her and affecting her marks.

There are pressures you have as parents, balancing normal life with the risks of an adventure. I think the most difficult aspect is the way this affects other members of your family. I am driven into adventures, and being a father does not stop me doing it. At the time, I am motivated, and actually I can brush off the pressures a bit easier. But I carry the guilt when I do it. On reflection, I am upset now thinking about it.

How could I behave like that?

Except that I know tomorrow, if I get driven to do something else, it will probably happen again.

I think I have regrets. I know I say, I am here on the planet for a short time, and there are challenges to be met, whether it be work or pleasure, I want to maximise the challenge. But I have family responsibilities.

Yet I could live another fifteen years and add no value by resisting every urge to have an adventure.

If I could live forever well, obviously, that would be a real bet, wouldn't it?

I think there is a point when my responsibilities start to fade. I help bring children into the world and help bring them up, educate them. Then one day they decide to go overseas. How often will I see them then?

They won't think about me, and why should they? They have a life to lead.

I have to carry on as an individual as well as a part of the family. I do not give up my own identity or aspirations just because I have other responsibilities.

It should be understood that the person I am is always going to be the person I am. I do not change. People do not really change. But that doesn't take away some of the pressure, either before or afterwards.

I think for a woman to behave the way Christina did was fantastic. If she really had been selfish, she would have told me before I went, and made it even more difficult for me.


Then again.....

My mother needed a heart operation. She went in for a routine check one week before I went to Kilimanjaro, and they said they could not release her. She was told she needed a double heart by-pass operation, but that she was too ill to have it. They suggested an alternative operation on three arteries, even though it was also dangerous.

We got called in as the family. Because the arteries were so close to the heart it was more dangerous than normal. I was meant to be flying out on the Thursday and my mother was having the operation on the Friday.

My mother knew I was going to Kilimanjaro. Had she felt I had cancelled the trip on her behalf it would have alarmed her, and made it seem the operation was more serious than it was.

My wife told me to go.

In this case it was in Africa, I had a phone, technically there would be a period when I was out of contact but if I needed to come back, I could come back. I could not do anything about my mother's operation.

There was nothing I could see that was going to prevent me going to Kilimanjaro.

I felt it was important for me to go there. Was it more important than my family? Obviously not. But it was not a case of either/or. It was only the family that had the potential to stop me in my tracks. But they did not do that.

My mother lived through a successful operation.

Would my family stop me in the future?

It would be arrogant to say no.

It would be a change if I said yes, so I do not know.

I would be surprised if I could not be persuasive enough to justify the next trip.

Do I know where the next trip is?

Baffin Island might be nice. It is a place that interests me. I would like to go there.